# LAW LIBRARY BENCHMARKS, 2020-21 EDITION

ISBN 978-1-57440-645-0 

## Contents

# THE QUESTIONNAIRE

1. Please give us the following contact information

   A. Name:
   B. Organization:
   C. Work Title:
   D. Country:
   E. Email Address:

2. Type of law library

   A. Law firm library
   B. University law library
   C. Courthouse library
   D. Non-Courthouse government agency nonprofit or international agency law library
   E. Private company law library
   F. Other (please specify)

3. Approximately how many librarians in FTE employees terms are employed by your library?

4. Current operating status of the library

   A. We have completely shut the library
   B. We have shut the library to physical traffic but have maintained online access
   C. We have kept the library open to patrons subject to social distancing and other virus containment measures
   D. We have not really made any major changes in terms of patron access

5. If you have fully or partially closed the library to patron access what changes will you make to re-open?

6. Your library staff has primarily used which of the following to interact with library patrons and staff at remote locations.

   A. Skype
   B. Zoom
   C. WebEx
   D. Google Hangouts
   E. Adobe Connect
   F. Microsoft Teams
   G. Other (please specify)

7. Have any employees of the library been quarantined, diagnosed with Covid-19 or passed away from the disease.

   A. Employees Quarantined
   B. Employees Diagnosed
   C. Employees Passed Away

8. Which phrase best describes the path that your organization is likely to take over the next three months as a response to the coronavirus epidemic?

   A. We do not plan to bring any employees back to the office in this period
   B. Most employees have worked from home and we expect to bring at least 25% back to the office
   C. Most employees have worked from home but we plan to bring at least 50% of them back to the office
   D. Most of our employees have worked from home but we expect to bring 75% back to the office
   E. Most of our employees have worked from home but we expect to bring them all back to the office
   F. Most employees have continued to work at the office during the crisis

9. How many other full time equivalent employees such as library assistants, technology staff, secretaries and others are employed by the library?

10. What single task or objective has taken an increasing amount of staff time in recent months and why has so much staff time been devoted to it?

11. What was or will be your library or parent organization's overall spending on staff salary costs, excluding benefits such as health insurance, in each of the following years:

    A. 2018
    B. 2019
    C. 2020

12. Which of the following best approximates your library's personnel plans over the next year?

    A. We plan to add overall staff
    B. We will freeze all hiring except for replacements for staff who leave
    C. We will freeze all hiring
    D. We will reduce overall staff

13. How do your view the economic impact of the coronavirus epidemic on the economic condition of your parent organization?

    A. It has been pretty devastating for us
    B. It's been seriously injurious
    C. It has hurt us in the short term
    D. It has not really affected us
    E. It has actually created new opportunities and revenues for us

14. What was the library's budget in each of the following years? (including spending for salaries)

    A. 2018
    B. 2019
    C. 2020 (anticipated)

15. If your library has made any substantial change to budget allocations over the few months, please briefly summarize these changes.

16. What was the library's total expenditures for content/materials in both print and electronic formats in each of the following years?
(Content is defined as books, journals, magazines, audio visual materials, newsletters, databases, directories and other such information vehicles)

A. 2018
B. 2019
C. 2020 (anticipated)

17. How much did the library spend for online databases in the following years?

A. 2018
B. 2019
C. 2020 (anticipated)

18. Over the next year do you feel that your law library will spend more, spend less, spend about the same, or continue not to use the following suppliers of legal information?

| | Spend More | Spend About the Same | Spend Less | Continue not to Use |
|---|---|---|---|---|
| Bloomberg | | | | |
| Thomson/Reuters/West | | | | |
| Reed/Elsevier/LexisNexis | | | | |
| Wolters/Kluwers/CHH | | | | |
| American Bar Association | | | | |

19. Which of the following do you feel has most reached out to help during the coronavirus epidemic?

A. LexisNexis
B. West/Thomson-Reuters
C. Bloomberg
D. Hein
E. FastCase
F. Google Scholar
G. Other (please specify)

20. How important do you feel it is to acquaint your library's end users with newly emerging automated and robotic methods of conducting legal information searches?

    A. Absolutely critical as it is the wave of the future
    B. Very important right now
    C. Important but not a big factor right now
    D. Useful perhaps but still more theoretical than actual
    E. Hyped a bit too much, not really a factor now
    F. Have not really heard about it and not asked about it at all

21. What steps has your library taken to familiarize your organization's librarians with artificial intelligence approaches to legal information searching?

22. Which law artificial intelligence products have been, or you think will be, most useful for your organization? Why?

23. How influential would you say that the law library is relative to the norm for other departments and agencies within your organization -- in its ability to protect its interests, particularly in budget negotiations?

    A. The Library is More Influential than the Norm for other Players
    B. The Library is About as Influential as the Norm for other Players
    C. The Library is Less Influential than the Norm for other Players

24. What tools does the library use to monitor how much various library databases, software and other tools are used by its patrons?

25. About how often do you present library tool usage data to organization executives outside of the law library? (i.e., law partners/management committee, university deans, government agency management, etc.)

    A. Monthly or More Frequently
    B. Every few months
    C. Every 6 months or so
    D. Annually
    E. Once every few years
    F. More or Less Never

26. What kind of help has your library received from your consortium in dealing with the impact of the coronavirus epidemic on the library?

27. How many subscriptions that require payment does the library maintain to legal journals in the following formats:

    A. Print with no Electronic Access:
    B. Electronic with no Print Counterpart:
    C. Both print and Electronic Access:

28. How much did (will) the library spend for print and/or electronic versions of legal, scientific and other scholarly and professional journals in:

    A. 2019
    B. 2020 (anticipated)

29. What are your expectations over the next three years for the library's print collection of journals and periodicals?

30. How much did (will) the library spend for print reporters in:

    A. 2019
    B. 2020

31. In general, how has the coronavirus epidemic impacted or will impact your print materials collection?

# PARTICIPANTS LIST

Akin Gump Strauss Hauer & Feld LLP
Bloomberg Industry Group
Burke, Williams & Sorensen LLP
CA Western School of Law
Case Western Reserve School of Law
Charleston School of Law
Chicago-Kent College of Law Library
Department of Justice Canada
DLA Piper (Canada) LLP
Frost Brown Todd LLC
Georgetown University Law Library
Gowling WLG (Canada)
Hawaii Supreme Court Law Library
Jones Day
Koffman Kalef LLP
Massachusetts Attorney General's Office
Mendocino County Law Library
Middlesex Law Library
Middleton Reutlinger
Miller Johnson
Milling Benson
Nevada Supreme Court Library
New York Law Institute
Nexsen Pruet, LLC
Rivkin Radler
San Diego Law Library
South Texas College of Law Houston
Supreme Court of Ohio
Thurgood Marshall Law Library
University of Maine School of Law
University of Colorado
University of Illinois

# Characteristics of the Sample

Type of law library

| | # |
|---|---|
| Law firm library | 15 |
| University law library | 10 |
| Courthouse library | 7 |
| Non-Courthouse government agency nonprofit or international agency law library | 3 |
| Total | 35 |

FTE employees

| | # |
|---|---|
| Less than 3 | 8 |
| 3 - 4 | 9 |
| 5 - 8 | 10 |
| More than 8 | 8 |
| Total | 35 |

Current operating status of the library

| | # |
|---|---|
| We have completely shut the library | 1 |
| We have shut the library to physical traffic but have maintained online access | 27 |
| We have kept the library open to patrons subject to social distancing and other virus containment measures | 4 |
| We have not really made any major changes in terms of patron access | 3 |
| Total | 35 |

# SUMMARY OF MAIN FINDINGS

## Current Plans to Alter Status or Re-open the Library

We asked: If you have fully or partially closed the library to patron access what changes will you make to re-open?

In general, law firm libraries were waiting for instructions from management. University librarians were somewhat more proactive, taking and planning steps to reduce concentrations of patrons, enhance social distancing, quarantine circulating materials, install plexiglass dividers, making cleaning materials and disinfectants highly available. They seem highly focused and communicate a sense of mission.

Courthouse libraries also seem to be more or less waiting for marching orders from above. Only the university law libraries seem to be showing a great deal of initiative perhaps reflecting their greater foot traffic and greater risks.

## Communications Technologies Used to Correspond with Patrons & Staff from a Distance

We asked what kind of technologies that the librarians were currently using (most are working remotely) to communicate with library patrons. First, we asked about Skype, which was being used only by 5.71% of libraries sampled. Zoom, on the other hand, was being used by 54.29% of respondents, including all of the university law libraries sampled.

20% of those sampled were using WebEx to interact with library patrons. 46.7% of law firms sampled were using WebEx and their use accounted for all of the use of WebEx by the libraries sampled. Only 5.71% were using Google Hangouts and none were using Adobe Connect.

17.4% were using Microsoft Teams with most usage by courthouse and other government law libraries. Some other programs mentioned include BlueJeans, GoToMeeting, Facetime and Google Meet.

## Employees Quarantined, Diagnosed or Passed Away Due to COVID-19

We asked: have any employees of the library been quarantined, diagnosed with Covid-19 or passed away from the disease?

The libraries sampled had quarantined a mean of 1.7 employees with a range of 0 to 19. None in the sample had been diagnosed with COVID-19 and none had passed away due to the disease.

## Patron Organization Plans to Being Back Employees to the Physical Workplace

We asked: Which phrase best describes the path that your organization is likely to take over the next three months as a response to the coronavirus epidemic?

We gave three choices for this multiple choice question which were: We do not plan to bring any employees back to the office in this period Most employees have worked from home and we expect to bring at least 25% back to the office Most employees have worked from home but we plan to bring at least 50% of them back to the office Most of our employees have worked from home but we expect to bring 75% back to the office Most of our employees have worked from home but we expect to bring them all back to the office Most employees have continued to work at the office during the crisis

A plurality of 31.43% chose "Most employees have worked from home and we expect to bring at least 25% back to the office." The second most common answer, given by 25.71%, was "Most of our employees have worked from home but we expect to bring them all back to the office."

## Current Number of Full Time Equivalent Employees of the Library

We asked: How many other full time equivalent employees such as library assistants, technology staff, secretaries and others are employed by the library?

The mean was 4.7 employees with a median of 2.5.

## Tasks or Objectives Consuming More Staff Time in Recent Months

We asked: What single task or objective has taken an increasing amount of staff time in recent months and why has so much staff time been devoted to it?

For law firm librarians, keeping up with new legislation and developments related to the pandemic accounted for much of their time. In addition, some libraries furloughed employees creating a greater workload for those still employed. Librarians are also taking closer looks at their vendor agreements and considering cuts in resources.

For university librarians, teaching online and obtaining online equivalents for print materials were factors in the workload.

## Spending on Salaries and Benefits 2018, 2019, 2020

What was or will be your library or parent organization's overall spending on staff salary costs (in US $), excluding benefits such as health insurance, in each of the following years: 2018, 2019, 2020?

The first year we asked about was 2018. Mean spending was $701,902 and it rose considerably to a mean of $753,229 in 2019, an increase of 7.3%. mostly driven by increases in government-related law libraries. Spending at law firm libraries for salaries was more or less flat while at university law libraries, it rose modestly, more or less in line with inflation. The librarians sampled did not project decrease in 2020 with mean spending again rising significantly, to a mean of $799,251, or by 6.1%.

Spending by law firm libraries dropped 6.23% but university law library spending once again rose modestly and courthouse and other government law libraries registered big spending increases, accounting for more or less all of the increase in spending by law libraries generally.

## Personnel Plans for the Upcoming Year

We asked about personnel plans for the next year, giving four potential answer to this multiple choice question; these were: We plan to add overall staff We will freeze all hiring except for replacements for staff who leave We will freeze all hiring We will reduce overall staff

Most plan some form of hiring freeze but only 11.43% plan to reduce staff while 8.57% plan to increase staff. Law firms and university law libraries accounted for all those planning to reduce staff.

## View of the Impact of the Pandemic on the Economic Health of the Parent Organization

We asked: How do your view the economic impact of the coronavirus epidemic on the economic condition of your parent organization?

We gave five possible answers to this multiple choice question. These were: It has been pretty devastating for us It's been seriously injurious It has hurt us in the short term It has not really affected us It has actually created new opportunities and revenues for us

A plurality of 45.71% chose "It has hurt us in the short term." University law school and courthouse libraries were the most likely to claim injury while most law firms saw it predominantly as something that hurt them in the short term.

## The Library Overall Budget, 2018, 2019 and 2020

We asked: What was the library's budget in US$ for 2018,2019 and 2020?

The mean for 2018 was $1.547 million, a figure which rose to $1.595 million in 2019, an increase of 3.1%. Budgets once again rose in 2020 but to only $1.633 million, or by 2.38%. Law firm budget fell slightly but by less than one half of one percent. University law library budgets in the sample fell most dramatically, declining from a mean of $1.478 million to $1.246 million or by 15,7%. But increases by government-related law libraries (perhaps related to stimulus spending?) led to an overall modest increase.

## Substantial Changes Made to Budget Allocations Over the Past Few Months, Post Pandemic Inception

We asked: If your library has made any substantial change to budget allocations over the few months, please briefly summarize these changes. Law firm libraries focused on reducing duplication of resources and in general with cutting print resources. Some experienced lay-offs and other saved on maintenance and utility bills. One university library moved to self-checkout and many placed holds on new print purchases.

Courthouse libraries are looking to cut costs in the upcoming fiscal year but seem somewhat safe at the moment.

## Library Spending on Content/Materials 2018, 2019 and 2020

We asked: What was the library's total expenditures (in US $) for content/materials in both print and electronic formats in each of the following years:(Content is defined as books, journals, magazines, audio visual materials, newsletters, databases, directories and other such information vehicles)

We asked about three years, 2018, 2019 and 2020. Mean spending in 2018 was $738, 205. It was flat in 2019, skipping up very slightly to a mean of $738, 760. It fell in 2020 to a mean of $727,224, a modest decline of 1.57%. University law libraries account for most of the drop, and their spending fell to a mean of $656,125 from $741,000 a year earlier, a significant drop of 11.5%.

## Library Spending for Online Databases 2018, 2019, 2020

We looked at spending specifically for online databases, once again asking about 2018, 2019 and 2020.

Mean spending in 2018 was $458,029, a figure which rose to $522, 813 in 2019 and then dropped just slightly to $518,557 in 2020. Perhaps the biggest story here is the big drop in law firm spending which dropped despite apparent efforts to replace print with online resources. Means spending fell from $747,840 in 2019 to $683,959 estimated for 2020, a drop of approximately 7.9%. University spending is expected to fall similarly, by about 7.2%.

## Plans for Spending on Specific Legal Information Suppliers

We asked: Over the next year do you feel that your law library will spend more, spend less, spend about the same, or continue not to use the following suppliers of legal information? We asked about the following publishers, each individually; they were: Bloomberg, Thomson, Reed/Lexis-Nexis, Wolters and the American Bar Association.

We gave four answers to this multiple choice question which were: Spend More Spend About the Same Spend Less Continue not to Use

More than 57% planned to spend the same amount on Bloomberg while 14.29% planned to spend less and none spend more

For Thomson/Reuters/West 71.43% planned to spend about the same, 20% less and 5.71%, more.

For Reed/Elsevier/Lexis-Nexis, 65.71% planned to spend about the same, 17.14% planned to spend less and 2.86%, more.

For Wolters/Kluwers/CCH

48.57% planned to spend about the same, 37.14% less and 2.86% more.

For content from the American Bar Association, 42.86% planned to spend about the same, 20% less and none, more.

## View of Which Publishers Reached Out the Most During the Pandemic

We asked: Which of the following do you feel has most reached out to help during the coronavirus epidemic?

We asked about a range of publishers including Lexis, West, Bloomberg, Hein, Fastcase and Google Scholar. Generally, Lexis/Nexis and West/Thomson-Reuters dominated.

## View of the Importance of AI in Legal Research

We asked: How important do you feel it is to acquaint your library's end users with newly emerging automated and robotic methods of conducting legal information searches?

We gave six possible answers to this multiple choice question. These were: Absolutely critical as it is the wave of the future Very important right now Important but not a big factor right now Useful perhaps but still more theoretical than actual Hyped a bit too much, not really a factor now Have not really heard about it and not asked about it at all

A plurality of 31.43% chose "Important but not a big factor now", while 22.86% each chose "Absolutely critical as it is the wave of the future", and "Very important right now."

Law firm libraries and university law libraries were more likely than others to considered automated or AI searching as particularly important.

## Steps Taken to Familiarize Library Patrons with AI in Legal Research

We asked: What steps has your library taken to familiarize your organization's librarians with artificial intelligence approaches to legal information searching?

This was an open-ended question and mostly introduction was through seminars, conferences, webinars, online training and vendor demos.

## Most Popular AI Products

We asked: Which law artificial intelligence products have been, or you think will be, most useful for your organization? Why?

Westlaw features were most often mentioned by the law firms sampled.

## Level of Influence of the Law Library Over Institutional Resources Vis a Vis Other Departments in your Organization

We asked: How influential would you say that the law library is relative to the norm for other departments and agencies within your organization -- in its ability to protect its interests, particularly in budget negotiations?

We gave three possible answers to this multiple choice question. These were: The Library is More Influential than the Norm for other Players The Library is About as Influential as the Norm for other Players The Library is Less Influential than the Norm for other Players

A majority of 62.86% felt that the library was more or less as influential as other departments while 14.29% thought it more influential and 11.43%, less.

## Library Methods of Monitoring Content Database Usage

We asked: What tools does the library use to monitor how much various library databases, software and other tools are used by its patrons?

For the most part monitoring is based on vendor statistics though some use reports from their own proxy server or Google Analytics; monthly billing reports are important data sources for law firms, and some libraries use ERM software. Check out stats, COUNTER and KnowledgeTracker were also cited.

## Frequency of Presentation to Management of Usage Data of Library Resources

We asked: About how often do you present library tool/database usage data to organization executives outside of the law library? (i.e., law partners/management committee, university deans, government agency management, etc.)

We gave six possible answers to this multiple choice question which were: monthly or more frequently, every few months, every 6 months or so, annually, once every few years, and more or less never

A plurality of 31.43% presented data annually while the second most common response was "more or less never" given by 22.56% of respondents.

We asked: What kind of help has your library received from your consortium in dealing with the impact of the coronavirus epidemic on the library?

Almost exclusively it was the academic law libraries that reported help from consortiums.

## Number of Subscriptions Maintained to Legal Journals in Print Formats

We asked: How many subscriptions that require payment does the library maintain to legal journals in the following formats? The first format considered was print with no accompanying electronic access. The mean was 26.94 with most accounted for by law firm libraries, which subscribed to a mean of 48.71. Smaller libraries were much more likely than larger ones to maintain print-alone access to journals.

## Number of Subscriptions Maintained to Legal Journals in Electronic Formats

The second format considered was electronic access with no corresponding print access. The mean number of subscriptions was 57.55. Most of this volume was accounted for by university law libraries which had a mean of 118.75 such subscriptions, followed by law firm libraries, which had a mean of 35.

## Number of Subscriptions Maintained to Legal Journals in Joint Print/Electronic Formats

The third format considered was both print and electronic access 13together. Libraries in the sample maintained a mean of 17.71 such journal subscriptions. University law libraries had the most such subscriptions , a mean of 28 followed by law firm libraries, with a mean of 15.

## Spending for Law Journals in 2019 and 2020

We asked: How much did the library spend (in US $) for print and/or electronic versions of legal, scientific and other scholarly and professional journals in 2019?

The mean was $127,327 with a range of 0 to $700,000. Expected spending for 2020 showed a dramatic drop to $110,772, a decline of 13%. Drops were mostly accounted for by university law libraries; their spending was expected to drop dramatically from a mean of $180,750 to a mean of $130,500, a fall of 27.8%.

We asked the open ended question: What are your expectations over the next three years for the library's print collection of journals and periodicals? In general, the trend towards reduced print expenditures should continue and accelerate.

## Spending for Print Reporters in 2019 and 2020

We asked: How much did (will) the library spend (in US $) for print reporters in 2019 and 2020?

In 2019 mean spending by the libraries in the sample was $47,054 with a range of 0 to $350,000. Spending by courthouse libraries, a mean of $175,300, accounts for much of the total, though university law libraries are still relatively heavy spenders, a mean of $62,500 in 2019.

Mean spending is expected to fall significantly in 2020 to a mean of $43,362 a fall of 10%. Courthouse libraries are still expected to spend heavily, with spending actually increasing to a mean of $203,300, an increase of 16%. But spending by law firms tumbles to a mean of $37,500 from $62,500 more than offsetting the increase by courthouse libraries in the sample.

## Impact of the Pandemic on Plans for the Print Materials Collection

In closing we asked: In general, how has the coronavirus epidemic impacted or will impact your print materials collection?

In general the move to online service re-affirmed.

If you have fully or partially closed the library to patron access what changes will you make to re-open? Broken out by Type of law library

Law firm library

1) We are a corporate library and the company will make that decision for us.
2) Nothing is planned for the moment.
3) It will be a Board decision, the Board members have been watching what the Courts have been doing as a guide, but as an independent body will make a final decision.
4) While shut down I go in once in a while to weed books.
5) staggered schedules - minimal hours
6) Our firm management will make the decisions about reopening. The warning is there will be a new normal. We are looking to make most books available online.
7) While the library is still technically open, everyone is working from home.
8) No changes, we are very small
9) limits of foot traffic Rotating staff schedule some in some working at home state WFH order extends int mid-June
10) Still to be determined.

University law library

1) Remove chairs to provide social distancing, require patrons and staff to wear masks, provide hand sanitizer, limit public access, reduce F2F transactions at service points, acquire a self-checkout system, institute policies and procedures to allow only 50 patrons in the library at one time, stagger working schedules so that staff can social distance.
2) Make masks, gloves, thermometers and hand sanitizer available; remove chairs for social distancing; install plexiglass barriers at service points; continue to have faculty and staff work at home as much as possible and offer reference via chat.
3) Limit patron categories to university community and create social distancing in the library.
4) We are putting in social distancing parameters all around the law library.
5) Among the other changes that we will make, we are looking to: reduce seats in to accommodate social distancing rules; make masks, gloves, hand sanitizer, and surface cleaning products widely available; installing plexiglass dividers at service stations; installing directional signs throughout all public spaces (e.g., designating some stairs as up and others as down); having more frequent cleaning; reconfigure uses where original use is not possible to accommodate with social distancing (e.g., group study rooms)

6) Gloves and Mask, limiting the number of entries, and controlling the flow of patrons to limit exposure.
7) Touchless pickup of Library checkouts Social distancing measures Disinfection routine
8) Limit to students, then public patrons. Limit the number of patrons in the building. Provide hand sanitizer.
9) The plans are not set yet. We are considering, sneeze guards at public desks, increased cleaning, cleaning wipes and additional antibacterial gel for the public. Turning off our study room reserve system. Rooms will be limited to one or two people, depending on the size. Only circulating titles that are not available online. Print materials that do circulate will be quarantined for 3 days. Reduce service hours. Staff will continue to meet virtual and remain at a distance.
10) This is still undecided. I am sure there will be limited seating, proper distance between carrels, protective barriers at service points.

Courthouse library

1) Directional tape
2) Unsure yet. We are thinking of still being closed to the public while allowing those that work in the building access to the collection.
3) We will wait for guidance from the building, court and state, and then use that to develop any changes we need to make for the library.
4) Rearrange the furniture, compel social distancing within the library, re-shelve the books after being used by our patrons, and wiping them down before doing so. No longer allowing patrons to operate the copy machine.
5) Ongoing discussions with management to determine how we will re-open to the public.
6) Finding ways to safely interact with the public, which will likely include wearing masks and gloves and somehow finding a way to maintain a safe distance yet remaining helpful
7) We are awaiting direction from our Chief Justice, our Governor, and City and County of Honolulu Mayor.

Non-Courthouse government agency nonprofit or international agency law library

1) We are presently formulating plans to reopen to staff first, then patrons. We do not yet have the specifics developed but we are looking at all safety options to keep staff and public healthy.
2) To be determined. Various options and scenarios are being discussed.
3) Will follow whatever guidelines are established by AGO management team

# Table 1 Your library staff has primarily used which of the following to interact with library patrons and staff at remote locations?

## Table 1.1.1 Has your library staff primarily used Skype to interact with library patrons and staff at remote locations?

| | No Answer | Yes | No |
|---|---|---|---|
| Entire sample | 22.86% | 5.71% | 71.43% |

## Table 1.1.2 Has your library staff primarily used Skype to interact with library patrons and staff at remote locations? Broken out by Type of law library

| Type of law library | No Answer | Yes | No |
|---|---|---|---|
| Law firm library | 33.33% | 6.67% | 60.00% |
| University law library | 0.00% | 10.00% | 90.00% |
| Courthouse library | 42.86% | 0.00% | 57.14% |
| Non-Courthouse government agency nonprofit or international agency law library | 0.00% | 0.00% | 100.00% |

## Table 1.1.3 Has your library staff primarily used Skype to interact with library patrons and staff at remote locations? Broken out by FTE employees

| FTE employees | No Answer | Yes | No |
|---|---|---|---|
| Less than 3 | 50.00% | 0.00% | 50.00% |
| 3 - 4 | 33.33% | 11.11% | 55.56% |
| 5 - 8 | 0.00% | 10.00% | 90.00% |
| More than 8 | 12.50% | 0.00% | 87.50% |

Table 1.1.4 Has your library staff primarily used Skype to interact with library patrons and staff at remote locations? Broken out by Current operating status of the library

| Current operating status of the library | No Answer | Yes | No |
|---|---|---|---|
| We have completely shut the library | 0.00% | 100.00% | 0.00% |
| We have shut the library to physical traffic but have maintained online access | 22.22% | 3.70% | 74.07% |
| We have kept the library open to patrons subject to social distancing and other virus containment measures | 50.00% | 0.00% | 50.00% |
| We have not really made any major changes in terms of patron access | 0.00% | 0.00% | 100.00% |

Table 1.2.1 Has your library staff primarily used Zoom to interact with library patrons and staff at remote locations

| | No Answer | Yes | No |
|---|---|---|---|
| Entire sample | 22.86% | 54.29% | 22.86% |

Table 1.2.2 Has your library staff primarily used Zoom to interact with library patrons and staff at remote locations Broken out by Type of law library

| Type of law library | No Answer | Yes | No |
|---|---|---|---|
| Law firm library | 33.33% | 33.33% | 33.33% |
| University law library | 0.00% | 100.00% | 0.00% |
| Courthouse library | 42.86% | 42.86% | 14.29% |
| Non-Courthouse government agency nonprofit or international agency law library | 0.00% | 33.33% | 66.67% |

Table 1.2.3 Has your library staff primarily used Zoom to interact with library patrons and staff at remote locations Broken out by FTE employees

| FTE employees | No Answer | Yes | No |
|---|---|---|---|
| Less than 3 | 50.00% | 37.50% | 12.50% |
| 3 - 4 | 33.33% | 33.33% | 33.33% |
| 5 - 8 | 0.00% | 80.00% | 20.00% |
| More than 8 | 12.50% | 62.50% | 25.00% |

Table 1.2.4 Has your library staff primarily used Zoom to interact with library patrons and staff at remote locations Broken out by Current operating status of the library

| Current operating status of the library | No Answer | Yes | No |
|---|---|---|---|
| We have completely shut the library | 0.00% | 100.00% | 0.00% |
| We have shut the library to physical traffic but have maintained online access | 22.22% | 55.56% | 22.22% |
| We have kept the library open to patrons subject to social distancing and other virus containment measures | 50.00% | 25.00% | 25.00% |
| We have not really made any major changes in terms of patron access | 0.00% | 66.67% | 33.33% |

Table 1.3.1 Has your library staff primarily used WebEx to interact with library patrons and staff at remote locations

| | No Answer | Yes | No |
|---|---|---|---|
| Entire sample | 22.86% | 20.00% | 57.14% |

Table 1.3.2 Has your library staff primarily used WebEx to interact with library patrons and staff at remote locations Broken out by Type of law library

| Type of law library | No Answer | Yes | No |
|---|---|---|---|
| Law firm library | 33.33% | 46.67% | 20.00% |
| University law library | 0.00% | 0.00% | 100.00% |
| Courthouse library | 42.86% | 0.00% | 57.14% |
| Non-Courthouse government agency nonprofit or international agency law library | 0.00% | 0.00% | 100.00% |

Table 1.3.3 Has your library staff primarily used WebEx to interact with library patrons and staff at remote locations Broken out by FTE employees

| FTE employees | No Answer | Yes | No |
|---|---|---|---|
| Less than 3 | 50.00% | 12.50% | 37.50% |
| 3 - 4 | 33.33% | 22.22% | 44.44% |
| 5 - 8 | 0.00% | 20.00% | 80.00% |
| More than 8 | 12.50% | 25.00% | 62.50% |

Table 1.3.4 Has your library staff primarily used WebEx to interact with library patrons and staff at remote locations Broken out by Current operating status of the library

| Current operating status of the library | No Answer | Yes | No |
|---|---|---|---|
| We have completely shut the library | 0.00% | 0.00% | 100.00% |
| We have shut the library to physical traffic but have maintained online access | 22.22% | 18.52% | 59.26% |
| We have kept the library open to patrons subject to social distancing and other virus containment measures | 50.00% | 25.00% | 25.00% |
| We have not really made any major changes in terms of patron access | 0.00% | 33.33% | 66.67% |

Table 1.4.1 Has your library staff primarily used Google Hangouts to interact with library patrons and staff at remote locations

| | No Answer | Yes | No |
|---|---|---|---|
| Entire sample | 22.86% | 5.71% | 71.43% |

Table 1.4.2 Has your library staff primarily used Google Hangouts to interact with library patrons and staff at remote locations Broken out by Type of law library

| Type of law library | No Answer | Yes | No |
|---|---|---|---|
| Law firm library | 33.33% | 0.00% | 66.67% |
| University law library | 0.00% | 10.00% | 90.00% |
| Courthouse library | 42.86% | 14.29% | 42.86% |
| Non-Courthouse government agency nonprofit or international agency law library | 0.00% | 0.00% | 100.00% |

Table 1.4.3 Has your library staff primarily used Google Hangouts to interact with library patrons and staff at remote locations Broken out by FTE employees

| FTE employees | No Answer | Yes | No |
|---|---|---|---|
| Less than 3 | 50.00% | 0.00% | 50.00% |
| 3 - 4 | 33.33% | 0.00% | 66.67% |
| 5 - 8 | 0.00% | 20.00% | 80.00% |
| More than 8 | 12.50% | 0.00% | 87.50% |

### Table 1.4.4 Has your library staff primarily used Google Hangouts to interact with library patrons and staff at remote locations Broken out by Current operating status of the library

| Current operating status of the library | No Answer | Yes | No |
|---|---|---|---|
| We have completely shut the library | 0.00% | 0.00% | 100.00% |
| We have shut the library to physical traffic but have maintained online access | 22.22% | 7.41% | 70.37% |
| We have kept the library open to patrons subject to social distancing and other virus containment measures | 50.00% | 0.00% | 50.00% |
| We have not really made any major changes in terms of patron access | 0.00% | 0.00% | 100.00% |

### Table 1.5.1 Has your library staff primarily used Adobe Connect to interact with library patrons and staff at remote locations

| | No Answer | Yes | No |
|---|---|---|---|
| Entire sample | 22.86% | 0.00% | 77.14% |

Table 1.6.1 Has your library staff primarily used Microsoft Teams to interact with library patrons and staff at remote locations

| | No Answer | Yes | No |
|---|---|---|---|
| Entire sample | 22.86% | 17.14% | 60.00% |

Table 1.6.2 Has your library staff primarily used Microsoft Teams to interact with library patrons and staff at remote locations Broken out by Type of law library

| Type of law library | No Answer | Yes | No |
|---|---|---|---|
| Law firm library | 33.33% | 13.33% | 53.33% |
| University law library | 0.00% | 10.00% | 90.00% |
| Courthouse library | 42.86% | 14.29% | 42.86% |
| Non-Courthouse government agency nonprofit or international agency law library | 0.00% | 66.67% | 33.33% |

Table 1.6.3 Has your library staff primarily used Microsoft Teams to interact with library patrons and staff at remote locations Broken out by FTE employees

| FTE employees | No Answer | Yes | No |
|---|---|---|---|
| Less than 3 | 50.00% | 12.50% | 37.50% |
| 3 - 4 | 33.33% | 11.11% | 55.56% |
| 5 - 8 | 0.00% | 30.00% | 70.00% |
| More than 8 | 12.50% | 12.50% | 75.00% |

Table 1.6.4 Has your library staff primarily used Microsoft Teams to interact with library patrons and staff at remote locations Broken out by Current operating status of the library

| Current operating status of the library | No Answer | Yes | No |
|---|---|---|---|
| We have completely shut the library | 0.00% | 0.00% | 100.00% |
| We have shut the library to physical traffic but have maintained online access | 22.22% | 18.52% | 59.26% |
| We have kept the library open to patrons subject to social distancing and other virus containment measures | 50.00% | 0.00% | 50.00% |
| We have not really made any major changes in terms of patron access | 0.00% | 33.33% | 66.67% |

Other:

1. We have remote desktop connections set up by our IT department.
2. Google Meet
3. Conference call
4. e-mail reference via KnowledgeTracker
5. Email & phone calls
6. Conference Call (while others on zoom)
7. email
8. Telephone and email as usual
9. phone and email only
10. Facetime
11. email
12. We do not have enough staff. I use email and the phone to communicate to people who assist me. Our firm has access to GoToMeeting if I need it.
13. iMessage
14. We're responding to incoming phone calls and e-mails.
15. BlueJeans for staff meetings, but we are not using any of these things to interact with library patrons. For patrons, we are using phone and email exclusively.

16. none
17. Considering Zoom
18. email
19. VPN into our network email, phones and messaging systems.

# Table 2 Have any employees of the library been quarantined, diagnosed with Covid-19 or passed away from the disease?

## Table 2.1.1 Have any employees of the library been quarantined?

| | Mean | Median | Minimum | Maximum |
|---|---|---|---|---|
| Entire sample | 1.70 | 0.00 | 0.00 | 19.00 |

## Table 2.1.2 Have any employees of the library been quarantined? Broken out by Type of law library

| Type of law library | Mean | Median | Minimum | Maximum |
|---|---|---|---|---|
| Law firm library | 0.00 | 0.00 | 0.00 | 0.00 |
| University law library | 5.43 | 0.00 | 0.00 | 19.00 |
| Courthouse library | 0.25 | 0.00 | 0.00 | 1.00 |
| Non-Courthouse government agency nonprofit or international agency law library | 0.00 | 0.00 | 0.00 | 0.00 |

## Table 2.1.3 Have any employees of the library been quarantined? Broken out by FTE employees

| FTE employees | Mean | Median | Minimum | Maximum |
|---|---|---|---|---|
| Less than 3 | 0.00 | 0.00 | 0.00 | 0.00 |
| 3 - 4 | 0.17 | 0.00 | 0.00 | 1.00 |
| 5 - 8 | 5.43 | 0.00 | 0.00 | 19.00 |
| More than 8 | 0.00 | 0.00 | 0.00 | 0.00 |

Table 2.1.4 Have any employees of the library been quarantined? Broken out by Current operating status of the library

| Current operating status of the library | Mean | Median | Minimum | Maximum |
|---|---|---|---|---|
| We have completely shut the library | 19.00 | 19.00 | 19.00 | 19.00 |
| We have shut the library to physical traffic but have maintained online access | 1.18 | 0.00 | 0.00 | 19.00 |
| We have kept the library open to patrons subject to social distancing and other virus containment measures | 0.00 | 0.00 | 0.00 | 0.00 |
| We have not really made any major changes in terms of patron access | 0.00 | 0.00 | 0.00 | 0.00 |

Table 2.2.1 Have any employees of the library been diagnosed?

| | Mean | Median | Minimum | Maximum |
|---|---|---|---|---|
| Entire sample | 0.00 | 0.00 | 0.00 | 0.00 |

Table 2.3.1 Have any employees of the library been passed away?

| | Mean | Median | Minimum | Maximum |
|---|---|---|---|---|
| Entire sample | 0.00 | 0.00 | 0.00 | 0.00 |

## Table 3.1 Which phrase best describes the path that your organization is likely to take over the next three months as a response to the coronavirus epidemic?

| | No Answer | We do not plan to bring any employees back to the office in this period | Most employees have worked from home and we expect to bring at least 25% back to the office | Most employees have worked from home but we plan to bring at least 50% of them back to the office | Most of our employees have worked from home but we expect to bring 75% back to the office | Most of our employees have worked from home but we expect to bring them all back to the office | Most employees have continued to work at the office during the crisis |
|---|---|---|---|---|---|---|---|
| Entire sample | 2.86% | 8.57% | 31.43% | 5.71% | 17.14% | 25.71% | 8.57% |

## Table 3.2 Which phrase best describes the path that your organization is likely to take over the next three months as a response to the coronavirus epidemic? Broken out by Type of law library

| Type of law library | No Answer | We do not plan to bring any employees back to the office in this period | Most employees have worked from home and we expect to bring at least 25% back to the office | Most employees have worked from home but we plan to bring at least 50% of them back to the office | Most of our employees have worked from home but we expect to bring 75% back to the office | Most of our employees have worked from home but we expect to bring them all back to the office | Most employees have continued to work at the office during the crisis |
|---|---|---|---|---|---|---|---|
| Law firm library | 6.67% | 0.00% | 26.67% | 6.67% | 20.00% | 26.67% | 13.33% |
| University law library | 0.00% | 30.00% | 30.00% | 0.00% | 10.00% | 30.00% | 0.00% |
| Courthouse library | 0.00% | 0.00% | 42.86% | 14.29% | 14.29% | 28.57% | 0.00% |
| Non-Courthouse government agency nonprofit or international agency law library | 0.00% | 0.00% | 33.33% | 0.00% | 33.33% | 0.00% | 33.33% |

## Table 3.3 Which phrase best describes the path that your organization is likely to take over the next three months as a response to the coronavirus epidemic? Broken out by FTE employees

| FTE employees | No Answer | We do not plan to bring any employees back to the office in this period | Most employees have worked from home and we expect to bring at least 25% back to the office | Most employees have worked from home but we plan to bring at least 50% of them back to the office | Most of our employees have worked from home but we expect to bring 75% back to the office | Most of our employees have worked from home but we expect to bring them all back to the office | Most employees have continued to work at the office during the crisis |
|---|---|---|---|---|---|---|---|
| Less than 3 | 0.00% | 0.00% | 25.00% | 0.00% | 25.00% | 37.50% | 12.50% |
| 3 - 4 | 0.00% | 0.00% | 22.22% | 11.11% | 11.11% | 44.44% | 11.11% |
| 5 - 8 | 0.00% | 30.00% | 50.00% | 10.00% | 10.00% | 0.00% | 0.00% |
| More than 8 | 12.50% | 0.00% | 25.00% | 0.00% | 25.00% | 25.00% | 12.50% |

## Table 3.4 Which phrase best describes the path that your organization is likely to take over the next three months as a response to the coronavirus epidemic? Broken out by Current operating status of the library

| Current operating status of the library | No Answer | We do not plan to bring any employees back to the office in this period | Most employees have worked from home and we expect to bring at least 25% back to the office | Most employees have worked from home but we plan to bring at least 50% of them back to the office | Most of our employees have worked from home but we expect to bring 75% back to the office | Most of our employees have worked from home but we expect to bring them all back to the office | Most employees have continued to work at the office during the crisis |
|---|---|---|---|---|---|---|---|
| We have completely shut the library | 0.00% | 100.00% | 0.00% | 0.00% | 0.00% | 0.00% | 0.00% |
| We have shut the library to physical traffic but have maintained online access | 3.70% | 7.41% | 37.04% | 7.41% | 14.81% | 22.22% | 7.41% |
| We have kept the library open to patrons subject to social distancing and other virus containment measures | 0.00% | 0.00% | 0.00% | 0.00% | 50.00% | 50.00% | 0.00% |
| We have not really made any major changes in terms of patron access | 0.00% | 0.00% | 33.33% | 0.00% | 0.00% | 33.33% | 33.33% |

## Table 4.1 How many other full time equivalent employees such as library assistants, technology staff, secretaries and others are employed by the library?

| | Mean | Median | Minimum | Maximum |
|---|---|---|---|---|
| Entire sample | 4.70 | 2.50 | 0.00 | 24.00 |

## Table 4.2 How many other full time equivalent employees such as library assistants, technology staff, secretaries and others are employed by the library? Broken out by Type of law library

| Type of law library | Mean | Median | Minimum | Maximum |
|---|---|---|---|---|
| Law firm library | 2.77 | 1.00 | 0.00 | 17.00 |
| University law library | 6.95 | 5.00 | 0.00 | 24.00 |
| Courthouse library | 3.79 | 2.50 | 0.00 | 15.00 |
| Non-Courthouse government agency nonprofit or international agency law library | 9.00 | 8.00 | 1.00 | 18.00 |

## Table 4.3 How many other full time equivalent employees such as library assistants, technology staff, secretaries and others are employed by the library? Broken out by FTE employees

| FTE employees | Mean | Median | Minimum | Maximum |
|---|---|---|---|---|
| Less than 3 | 0.38 | 0.00 | 0.00 | 1.00 |
| 3 - 4 | 4.06 | 2.00 | 0.00 | 15.00 |
| 5 - 8 | 4.10 | 4.50 | 0.00 | 11.00 |
| More than 8 | 10.50 | 7.50 | 2.00 | 24.00 |

## Table 4.4 How many other full time equivalent employees such as library assistants, technology staff, secretaries and others are employed by the library? Broken out by Current operating status of the library

| Current operating status of the library | Mean | Median | Minimum | Maximum |
|---|---|---|---|---|
| We have completely shut the library | 5.00 | 5.00 | 5.00 | 5.00 |
| We have shut the library to physical traffic but have maintained online access | 5.78 | 4.00 | 0.00 | 24.00 |
| We have kept the library open to patrons subject to social distancing and other virus containment measures | 0.88 | 1.00 | 0.00 | 1.50 |
| We have not really made any major changes in terms of patron access | 0.00 | 0.00 | 0.00 | 0.00 |

## What single task or objective has taken an increasing amount of staff time in recent months and why has so much staff time been devoted to it? Broken out by Type of law library

Law firm library

1) Processing incoming paper resources as we have them placed in a quarantine chamber for 4 days and then spray them as they build up.
2) Research on impacts on the economy resulting from Covid-19, and urgency of those requests.
3) Legislative monitoring due the critical legislation being passed right now due to the pandemic.
4) Current awareness. Constantly evolving legal and industry-related developments across many jurisdictions makes for a lot of work.
5) Catching up with Gov Docs. The Gov Docs person was out an extended period, so during the closure, working one day a week with other staff adding 3 days a week and whittling down the backlog.
6) I am completely going over each book and making sure the best up to date books are on the shelves.
7) Two of our staff have been furloughed so we have been re-assigning duties and streamlining procedures and outsourcing some duties.
8) research - takes a bit longer now and guiding the attorneys as they work from home.
9) 1 FTE employees library clerk was laid off so I, the remaining 1 FTE employees librarian am doing all library related tasks
10) troubleshooting IP-authenticated access to resources through Citrix, providing non-IP-authenticated alternative access points
11) Working on converting our book subscriptions to online access.
12) COVID-19 updates - source of major interest to our clients
13) we are very small, we never have more than 1 person in the Library area at a time.
14) For my department it has been budgeting review and vendor relations. We are taking another look at the duplicative formats for information, specifically those in print when we have digital/online options. We have been receiving a huge increase in vendor emails and phone calls regarding support, sales, and invoice/statement payments (even prior to the invoices being due).

University law library

1) Teaching online; Course planning, management, and providing student feedback has required more time than teaching F2F

2) Online communication about work tasks has increased because librarians are also working from home.
3) None.
4) It would have to be technology staff for our law faculty simply because all the courses have gone virtual.
5) Obtaining digital equivalents or alternatives to requested items typically available only in physical form
6) Mail, billing, and invoicing. it requires coordination with other departments at the law schools.
7) Obtaining online resources for patrons to replace our print collection during lockdown.
8) There are 2. Ensuring access to course books and study aids electronically. So that students have all the resources they can while offsite. The other is printing student requests. Students want print materials for their open book exams and are not allowed on campus. The library staff has been printing requests and letting the students pick them up curbside.
9) Teaching Advanced Legal Research course--getting up to speed on the technology and converting to online instruction is what has increased the staff time.

Courthouse library

1) Processing mail
2) Nothing. We were ready to operate outside of the building, had a Continuity of Operations Plan in effect, and handled the transition seamlessly.
3) Invoice processing is a lot harder to do remotely, putting together all of the pieces (invoices, POs, receipts) using Adobe.
4) Nothing out of the usual.
5) We may be migrating to a new cataloging system. We have to review all serials records and update them to have more consistency.
6) Mail and loose-leaf filings. We still have staff and librarians going into the library to handle mail that has not stopped with the pandemic. We still have to keep up with loose-leaf filing, otherwise, we'll never catch up once we return to the office.
7) Virtual/Remote access to library services and resources, so that we can continue to support the Judiciary and the public with legal information and reference questions.

Non-Courthouse government agency nonprofit or international agency law library

1) Projects to increase library outreach in terms of creating clinic space; outreach and staffing at public library partners; increasing Spanish language materials. Staff time devoted due to funding and our commitment to Access to Justice.

2) Obtaining electronic resources for material that was previously used in print format. Staff time has been devoted to contacting publishers/vendors for pricing and package options, setting up and training clients to use required technology (such as Adobe Digital Editions), investigating whether certain publications are available digitally, etc.
3) Getting invoices ready for approval by Budget division. Process for getting paper-only invoices scanned, emailed, signed, and sent to Accounts Payable has not been fully streamlined.

# Table 5 What was or will be your library or parent organization's overall spending on staff salary costs (in US $), excluding benefits such as health insurance, in each of the following years: 2018, 2019 and 2020?

## Table 5.1.1 What was or will be your library or parent organization's overall spending on staff salary costs (in US $), excluding benefits such as health insurance, in 2018?

| | Mean | Median | Minimum | Maximum |
|---|---|---|---|---|
| Entire sample | 701908.62 | 725000.00 | 40000.00 | 1451483.00 |

## Table 5.1.2 What was or will be your library or parent organization's overall spending on staff salary costs (in US $), excluding benefits such as health insurance, in 2018? Broken out by Type of law library

| Type of law library | Mean | Median | Minimum | Maximum |
|---|---|---|---|---|
| Law firm library | 382000.00 | 310000.00 | 40000.00 | 725000.00 |
| University law library | 752653.25 | 739806.50 | 531000.00 | 1000000.00 |
| Courthouse library | 745000.00 | 745000.00 | 590000.00 | 900000.00 |
| Non-Courthouse government agency nonprofit or international agency law library | 1357099.50 | 1357099.50 | 1262716.00 | 1451483.00 |

Table 5.1.3 What was or will be your library or parent organization's overall spending on staff salary costs (in US $), excluding benefits such as health insurance, in 2018? Broken out by FTE employees

| FTE employees | Mean | Median | Minimum | Maximum |
|---|---|---|---|---|
| Less than 3 | 40000.00 | 40000.00 | 40000.00 | 40000.00 |
| 3 - 4 | 467500.00 | 455000.00 | 235000.00 | 725000.00 |
| 5 - 8 | 720122.60 | 729613.00 | 531000.00 | 1000000.00 |
| More than 8 | 1204733.00 | 1262716.00 | 900000.00 | 1451483.00 |

Table 5.1.4 What was or will be your library or parent organization's overall spending on staff salary costs (in US $), excluding benefits such as health insurance, in 2018? Broken out by Current operating status of the library

| Current operating status of the library | Mean | Median | Minimum | Maximum |
|---|---|---|---|---|
| We have completely shut the library | 1000000.00 | 1000000.00 | 1000000.00 | 1000000.00 |
| We have shut the library to physical traffic but have maintained online access | 837756.89 | 729613.00 | 531000.00 | 1451483.00 |
| We have kept the library open to patrons subject to social distancing and other virus containment measures | 272500.00 | 272500.00 | 235000.00 | 310000.00 |
| We have not really made any major changes in terms of patron access | 40000.00 | 40000.00 | 40000.00 | 40000.00 |

Table 5.2.1 What was or will be your library or parent organization's overall spending on staff salary costs (in US $), excluding benefits such as health insurance, in 2019?

| | Mean | Median | Minimum | Maximum |
|---|---|---|---|---|
| Entire sample | 753229.08 | 675000.00 | 45000.00 | 1920246.00 |

Table 5.2.2 What was or will be your library or parent organization's overall spending on staff salary costs (in US $), excluding benefits such as health insurance, in 2019? Broken out by Type of law library

| Type of law library | Mean | Median | Minimum | Maximum |
|---|---|---|---|---|
| Law firm library | 385000.00 | 365000.00 | 45000.00 | 675000.00 |
| University law library | 731257.75 | 755515.50 | 514000.00 | 900000.00 |
| Courthouse library | 803500.00 | 803500.00 | 607000.00 | 1000000.00 |
| Non-Courthouse government agency nonprofit or international agency law library | 1667473.50 | 1667473.50 | 1414701.00 | 1920246.00 |

Table 5.2.3 What was or will be your library or parent organization's overall spending on staff salary costs (in US $), excluding benefits such as health insurance, in 2019? Broken out by FTE employees

| FTE employees | Mean | Median | Minimum | Maximum |
|---|---|---|---|---|
| Less than 3 | 45000.00 | 45000.00 | 45000.00 | 45000.00 |
| 3 - 4 | 470000.00 | 482500.00 | 240000.00 | 675000.00 |
| 5 - 8 | 706406.20 | 751031.00 | 514000.00 | 900000.00 |
| More than 8 | 1444982.33 | 1414701.00 | 1000000.00 | 1920246.00 |

Table 5.2.4 What was or will be your library or parent organization's overall spending on staff salary costs (in US $), excluding benefits such as health insurance, in 2019? Broken out by Current operating status of the library

| Current operating status of the library | Mean | Median | Minimum | Maximum |
|---|---|---|---|---|
| We have completely shut the library | 900000.00 | 900000.00 | 900000.00 | 900000.00 |
| We have shut the library to physical traffic but have maintained online access | 915775.33 | 751031.00 | 514000.00 | 1920246.00 |
| We have kept the library open to patrons subject to social distancing and other virus containment measures | 302500.00 | 302500.00 | 240000.00 | 365000.00 |
| We have not really made any major changes in terms of patron access | 45000.00 | 45000.00 | 45000.00 | 45000.00 |

Table 5.3.1 What was or will be your library or parent organization's overall spending on staff salary costs (in US $), excluding benefits such as health insurance, in 2020?

| | Mean | Median | Minimum | Maximum |
|---|---|---|---|---|
| Entire sample | 799251.23 | 635000.00 | 50000.00 | 2269704.00 |

Table 5.3.2 What was or will be your library or parent organization's overall spending on staff salary costs (in US $), excluding benefits such as health insurance, in 2020? Broken out by Type of law library

| Type of law library | Mean | Median | Minimum | Maximum |
|---|---|---|---|---|
| Law firm library | 361600.00 | 390000.00 | 50000.00 | 600000.00 |
| University law library | 766140.50 | 822281.00 | 520000.00 | 900000.00 |
| Courthouse library | 867500.00 | 867500.00 | 635000.00 | 1100000.00 |
| Non-Courthouse government agency nonprofit or international agency law library | 1891352.00 | 1891352.00 | 1513000.00 | 2269704.00 |

Table 5.3.3 What was or will be your library or parent organization's overall spending on staff salary costs (in US $), excluding benefits such as health insurance, in 2020? Broken out by FTE employees

| FTE employees | Mean | Median | Minimum | Maximum |
|---|---|---|---|---|
| Less than 3 | 50000.00 | 50000.00 | 50000.00 | 50000.00 |
| 3 - 4 | 439500.00 | 457500.00 | 243000.00 | 600000.00 |
| 5 - 8 | 739912.40 | 744562.00 | 520000.00 | 900000.00 |
| More than 8 | 1627568.00 | 1513000.00 | 1100000.00 | 2269704.00 |

Table 5.3.4 What was or will be your library or parent organization's overall spending on staff salary costs (in US $), excluding benefits such as health insurance, in 2020? Broken out by Current operating status of the library

| Current operating status of the library | Mean | Median | Minimum | Maximum |
|---|---|---|---|---|
| We have completely shut the library | 900000.00 | 900000.00 | 900000.00 | 900000.00 |
| We have shut the library to physical traffic but have maintained online access | 978585.11 | 744562.00 | 520000.00 | 2269704.00 |
| We have kept the library open to patrons subject to social distancing and other virus containment measures | 316500.00 | 316500.00 | 243000.00 | 390000.00 |
| We have not really made any major changes in terms of patron access | 50000.00 | 50000.00 | 50000.00 | 50000.00 |

## Table 6.1 Which of the following best approximates your library's personnel plans over the next year?

| | No Answer | We plan to add overall staff | We will freeze all hiring except for replacements for staff who leave | We will freeze all hiring | We will reduce overall staff |
|---|---|---|---|---|---|
| Entire sample | 5.71% | 8.57% | 31.43% | 42.86% | 11.43% |

## Table 6.2 Which of the following best approximates your library's personnel plans over the next year? Broken out by Type of law library

| Type of law library | No Answer | We plan to add overall staff | We will freeze all hiring except for replacements for staff who leave | We will freeze all hiring | We will reduce overall staff |
|---|---|---|---|---|---|
| Law firm library | 6.67% | 13.33% | 20.00% | 46.67% | 13.33% |
| University law library | 0.00% | 0.00% | 40.00% | 40.00% | 20.00% |
| Courthouse library | 14.29% | 0.00% | 42.86% | 42.86% | 0.00% |
| Non-Courthouse government agency nonprofit or international agency law library | 0.00% | 33.33% | 33.33% | 33.33% | 0.00% |

## Table 6.3 Which of the following best approximates your library's personnel plans over the next year? Broken out by FTE employees

| FTE employees | No Answer | We plan to add overall staff | We will freeze all hiring except for replacements for staff who leave | We will freeze all hiring | We will reduce overall staff |
|---|---|---|---|---|---|
| Less than 3 | 25.00% | 12.50% | 12.50% | 37.50% | 12.50% |
| 3 - 4 | 0.00% | 0.00% | 55.56% | 33.33% | 11.11% |
| 5 - 8 | 0.00% | 0.00% | 40.00% | 50.00% | 10.00% |
| More than 8 | 0.00% | 25.00% | 12.50% | 50.00% | 12.50% |

## Table 6.4 Which of the following best approximates your library's personnel plans over the next year? Broken out by Current operating status of the library

| Current operating status of the library | No Answer | We plan to add overall staff | We will freeze all hiring except for replacements for staff who leave | We will freeze all hiring | We will reduce overall staff |
|---|---|---|---|---|---|
| We have completely shut the library | 0.00% | 0.00% | 0.00% | 0.00% | 100.00% |
| We have shut the library to physical traffic but have maintained online access | 3.70% | 7.41% | 37.04% | 44.44% | 7.41% |
| We have kept the library open to patrons subject to social distancing and other virus containment measures | 0.00% | 25.00% | 25.00% | 25.00% | 25.00% |
| We have not really made any major changes in terms of patron access | 33.33% | 0.00% | 0.00% | 66.67% | 0.00% |

## Table 7.1 How do your view the economic impact of the coronavirus epidemic on the economic condition of your parent organization?

| | | | | | |
|---|---|---|---|---|---|
| Entire sample | 8.57% | 22.86% | 45.71% | 14.29% | 8.57% |

## Table 7.2 How do your view the economic impact of the coronavirus epidemic on the economic condition of your parent organization? Broken out by Type of law library

| Type of law library | It has been pretty devastating for us | It's been seriously injurious | It has hurt us in the short term | It has not really affected us | It has actually created new opportunities and revenues for us |
|---|---|---|---|---|---|
| Law firm library | 0.00% | 6.67% | 60.00% | 13.33% | 20.00% |
| University law library | 0.00% | 50.00% | 40.00% | 10.00% | 0.00% |
| Courthouse library | 42.86% | 14.29% | 28.57% | 14.29% | 0.00% |
| Non-Courthouse government agency nonprofit or international agency law library | 0.00% | 33.33% | 33.33% | 33.33% | 0.00% |

## Table 7.3 How do your view the economic impact of the coronavirus epidemic on the economic condition of your parent organization? Broken out by FTE employees

| FTE employees | It has been pretty devastating for us | It's been seriously injurious | It has hurt us in the short term | It has not really affected us | It has actually created new opportunities and revenues for us |
|---|---|---|---|---|---|
| Less than 3 | 12.50% | 0.00% | 62.50% | 25.00% | 0.00% |
| 3 - 4 | 11.11% | 22.22% | 55.56% | 11.11% | 0.00% |
| 5 - 8 | 0.00% | 40.00% | 40.00% | 10.00% | 10.00% |
| More than 8 | 12.50% | 25.00% | 25.00% | 12.50% | 25.00% |

## Table 7.4 How do your view the economic impact of the coronavirus epidemic on the economic condition of your parent organization? Broken out by Current operating status of the library

| Current operating status of the library | It has been pretty devastating for us | It's been seriously injurious | It has hurt us in the short term | It has not really affected us | It has actually created new opportunities and revenues for us |
|---|---|---|---|---|---|
| We have completely shut the library | 0.00% | 100.00% | 0.00% | 0.00% | 0.00% |
| We have shut the library to physical traffic but have maintained online access | 11.11% | 22.22% | 44.44% | 11.11% | 11.11% |
| We have kept the library open to patrons subject to social distancing and other virus containment measures | 0.00% | 25.00% | 50.00% | 25.00% | 0.00% |
| We have not really made any major changes in terms of patron access | 0.00% | 0.00% | 66.67% | 33.33% | 0.00% |

# Table 8 What was the library's budget (in US $) in each of the following years: (including spending for salaries) 2018, 2019 and 2020?

## Table 8.1.1 What was the library's budget (in US $) in 2018?

| | Mean | Median | Minimum | Maximum |
|---|---|---|---|---|
| Entire sample | 1546797.12 | 1300000.00 | 50000.00 | 5191483.00 |

## Table 8.1.2 What was the library's budget (in US $) in 2018? Broken out by Type of law library

| Type of law library | Mean | Median | Minimum | Maximum |
|---|---|---|---|---|
| Law firm library | 976085.43 | 1100000.00 | 80000.00 | 1677598.00 |
| University law library | 1620250.00 | 1800000.00 | 881000.00 | 2000000.00 |
| Courthouse library | 1284750.00 | 1194500.00 | 50000.00 | 2700000.00 |
| Non-Courthouse government agency nonprofit or international agency law library | 3921476.50 | 3921476.50 | 2651470.00 | 5191483.00 |

## Table 8.1.3 What was the library's budget (in US $) in 2018? Broken out by FTE employees

| FTE employees | Mean | Median | Minimum | Maximum |
|---|---|---|---|---|
| Less than 3 | 193333.33 | 80000.00 | 50000.00 | 450000.00 |
| 3 - 4 | 1250649.50 | 1200000.00 | 925000.00 | 1677598.00 |
| 5 - 8 | 1428333.33 | 1335000.00 | 881000.00 | 2000000.00 |
| More than 8 | 3035738.25 | 2675735.00 | 1600000.00 | 5191483.00 |

Table 8.1.4 What was the library's budget (in US $) in 2018? Broken out by Current operating status of the library

| Current operating status of the library | Mean | Median | Minimum | Maximum |
|---|---|---|---|---|
| We have completely shut the library | 2000000.00 | 2000000.00 | 2000000.00 | 2000000.00 |
| We have shut the library to physical traffic but have maintained online access | 1633688.69 | 1300000.00 | 50000.00 | 5191483.00 |
| We have kept the library open to patrons subject to social distancing and other virus containment measures | 1488799.00 | 1488799.00 | 1300000.00 | 1677598.00 |
| We have not really made any major changes in terms of patron access | 80000.00 | 80000.00 | 80000.00 | 80000.00 |

Table 8.2.1 What was the library's budget (in US $) in 2019?

| | Mean | Median | Minimum | Maximum |
|---|---|---|---|---|
| Entire sample | 1595185.06 | 1385000.00 | 50000.00 | 5660246.00 |

Table 8.2.2 What was the library's budget (in US $) in 2019? Broken out by Type of law library

| Type of law library | Mean | Median | Minimum | Maximum |
|---|---|---|---|---|
| Law firm library | 1064600.00 | 1100000.00 | 100000.00 | 2000000.00 |
| University law library | 1478250.00 | 1650000.00 | 813000.00 | 1800000.00 |
| Courthouse library | 1338500.00 | 1202000.00 | 50000.00 | 2900000.00 |
| Non-Courthouse government agency nonprofit or international agency law library | 4199473.00 | 4199473.00 | 2738700.00 | 5660246.00 |

Table 8.2.3 What was the library's budget (in US $) in 2019? Broken out by FTE employees

| FTE employees | Mean | Median | Minimum | Maximum |
|---|---|---|---|---|
| Less than 3 | 206666.67 | 100000.00 | 50000.00 | 470000.00 |
| 3 - 4 | 1420550.00 | 1416100.00 | 850000.00 | 2000000.00 |
| 5 - 8 | 1336166.67 | 1292500.00 | 813000.00 | 1800000.00 |
| More than 8 | 3199736.50 | 2819350.00 | 1500000.00 | 5660246.00 |

Table 8.2.4 What was the library's budget (in US $) in 2019? Broken out by Current operating status of the library

| Current operating status of the library | Mean | Median | Minimum | Maximum |
|---|---|---|---|---|
| We have completely shut the library | 1800000.00 | 1800000.00 | 1800000.00 | 1800000.00 |
| We have shut the library to physical traffic but have maintained online access | 1652765.08 | 1200000.00 | 50000.00 | 5660246.00 |
| We have kept the library open to patrons subject to social distancing and other virus containment measures | 1866100.00 | 1866100.00 | 1732200.00 | 2000000.00 |
| We have not really made any major changes in terms of patron access | 100000.00 | 100000.00 | 100000.00 | 100000.00 |

Table 8.3.1 What will be the library's budget (in US $) in 2020 (anticipated)?

| | Mean | Median | Minimum | Maximum |
|---|---|---|---|---|
| Entire sample | 1633047.94 | 1150000.00 | 120000.00 | 6009704.00 |

Table 8.3.2 What will be the library's budget (in US $) in 2020 (anticipated)? Broken out by Type of law library

| Type of law library | Mean | Median | Minimum | Maximum |
|---|---|---|---|---|
| Law firm library | 1059901.57 | 1050000.00 | 120000.00 | 2200000.00 |
| University law library | 1245500.00 | 1200000.00 | 782000.00 | 1800000.00 |
| Courthouse library | 1504750.00 | 1209500.00 | 500000.00 | 3100000.00 |
| Non-Courthouse government agency nonprofit or international agency law library | 4670752.00 | 4670752.00 | 3331800.00 | 6009704.00 |

Table 8.3.3 What will be the library's budget (in US $) in 2020 (anticipated)? Broken out by FTE employees

| FTE employees | Mean | Median | Minimum | Maximum |
|---|---|---|---|---|
| Less than 3 | 340000.00 | 400000.00 | 120000.00 | 500000.00 |
| 3 - 4 | 1437327.75 | 1412155.50 | 725000.00 | 2200000.00 |
| 5 - 8 | 1241833.33 | 1225000.00 | 782000.00 | 1800000.00 |
| More than 8 | 3385376.00 | 3215900.00 | 1100000.00 | 6009704.00 |

Table 8.3.4 What will be the library's budget (in US $) in 2020 (anticipated)? Broken out by Current operating status of the library

| Current operating status of the library | Mean | Median | Minimum | Maximum |
|---|---|---|---|---|
| We have completely shut the library | 1800000.00 | 1800000.00 | 1800000.00 | 1800000.00 |
| We have shut the library to physical traffic but have maintained online access | 1682115.69 | 1100000.00 | 400000.00 | 6009704.00 |
| We have kept the library open to patrons subject to social distancing and other virus containment measures | 1987155.50 | 1987155.50 | 1774311.00 | 2200000.00 |
| We have not really made any major changes in terms of patron access | 120000.00 | 120000.00 | 120000.00 | 120000.00 |

## If your library has made any substantial change to budget allocations over the few months, please briefly summarize these changes. Broken out by Type of law library

Law firm library

1) NA
2) Loss of two staff members with no replacements.
3) Cancellation of LexisNexis Quicklaw
4) Cut some of our databases for a two month period. Have cut back on janitorial and similar services. Have seen the electric bills drop
5) I have begun to cut print material from Library that is not used as much. We also no longer have and ESTATE section and those books have been cut.
6) Two employees furloughed without pay. Newspapers canceled for the most part as few are allowed in the office. Other print taken off standing order.
7) we have always tried to consolidate and pare down duplication
8) 1 of 2 FTE employees was laid off permanently by the parent organization
9) continuing to move allocations over to online resources rather than print
10) None at this time.
11) n/a
12) Reviewing and decreasing the duplication of resources.

University law library

1) We are moving to self-checkout in order to reduce the hours of part-time graduate student staff at the circulation desk.
2) Severe materials cut and probable lay-off of two people.
3) Just shifting costs more to digital items than physical items.
4) Hold on all print purchasing. No textbook purchases for the summer. No new purchases. hold on all standing orders.
5) none/unknown
6) NA
7) Budget has remained the same.

Courthouse library

1) We are cutting many print subscriptions.
2) Not yet. Looking at various online database contracts and hardcopy expenditures.
3) We will be seeing about, (estimated) 90% decrease in funding. We may have to drop all of our online resources.

4) No changes for us in current fiscal year, but the law library will be asked to cut $60,000 next fiscal year, and an as-yet to be determined amount for the fiscal year after that
5) Looked for any place to cut costs.

Non-Courthouse government agency nonprofit or international agency law library

1) We have requested our board allow the library to use reserves to meet expected shortfall in filing fee income over the next 3 months. We are also delaying preparing the budget for the next fiscal year as we see if filing fee income recovers when courts reopen in our state.
2) No changes in last  months, but anticipate changes when new FY begins on 1 July 2020

## Table 9 What was the library's total expenditures (in US $) for content/materials in both print and electronic formats in each of the following years: 2018, 2019 and 2020? (Content is defined as books, journals, magazines, audio visual materials, newsletters, databases, directories and other such information vehicles)

### Table 9.1.1 What were the library's total expenditures (in US $) for content/materials in both print and electronic formats in 2018?

| | Mean | Median | Minimum | Maximum |
|---|---|---|---|---|
| Entire sample | 738205.29 | 500000.00 | 2000.00 | 3740000.00 |

### Table 9.1.2 What were the library's total expenditures (in US $) for content/materials in both print and electronic formats in 2018? Broken out by Type of law library

| Type of law library | Mean | Median | Minimum | Maximum |
|---|---|---|---|---|
| Law firm library | 549933.00 | 440000.00 | 2000.00 | 1367598.00 |
| University law library | 773875.00 | 900250.00 | 295000.00 | 1000000.00 |
| Courthouse library | 473750.00 | 562500.00 | 25000.00 | 745000.00 |
| Non-Courthouse government agency nonprofit or international agency law library | 1419797.33 | 339392.00 | 180000.00 | 3740000.00 |

Table 9.1.3 What were the library's total expenditures (in US $) for content/materials in both print and electronic formats in 2018? Broken out by FTE employees

| FTE employees | Mean | Median | Minimum | Maximum |
|---|---|---|---|---|
| Less than 3 | 195000.00 | 180000.00 | 25000.00 | 380000.00 |
| 3 - 4 | 492399.50 | 300000.00 | 2000.00 | 1367598.00 |
| 5 - 8 | 702583.33 | 822500.00 | 295000.00 | 950000.00 |
| More than 8 | 1444848.00 | 850000.00 | 339392.00 | 3740000.00 |

Table 9.1.4 What were the library's total expenditures (in US $) for content/materials in both print and electronic formats in 2018? Broken out by Current operating status of the library

| Current operating status of the library | Mean | Median | Minimum | Maximum |
|---|---|---|---|---|
| We have completely shut the library | 900000.00 | 900000.00 | 900000.00 | 900000.00 |
| We have shut the library to physical traffic but have maintained online access | 727278.00 | 462500.00 | 2000.00 | 3740000.00 |
| We have kept the library open to patrons subject to social distancing and other virus containment measures | 733799.00 | 733799.00 | 100000.00 | 1367598.00 |

Table 9.2.1 What were the library's total expenditures (in US $) for content/materials in both print and electronic formats in 2019?

| | Mean | Median | Minimum | Maximum |
|---|---|---|---|---|
| Entire sample | 738759.82 | 500000.00 | 1000.00 | 3740000.00 |

Table 9.2.2 What were the library's total expenditures (in US $) for content/materials in both print and electronic formats in 2019? Broken out by Type of law library

| Type of law library | Mean | Median | Minimum | Maximum |
|---|---|---|---|---|
| Law firm library | 543366.67 | 442500.00 | 1000.00 | 1367200.00 |
| University law library | 741000.00 | 875000.00 | 314000.00 | 900000.00 |
| Courthouse library | 509750.00 | 607000.00 | 25000.00 | 800000.00 |
| Non-Courthouse government agency nonprofit or international agency law library | 1431905.67 | 370717.00 | 185000.00 | 3740000.00 |

Table 9.2.3 What were the library's total expenditures (in US $) for content/materials in both print and electronic formats in 2019? Broken out by FTE employees

| FTE employees | Mean | Median | Minimum | Maximum |
|---|---|---|---|---|
| Less than 3 | 198333.33 | 185000.00 | 25000.00 | 385000.00 |
| 3 - 4 | 490050.00 | 296000.00 | 1000.00 | 1367200.00 |
| 5 - 8 | 698833.33 | 810000.00 | 314000.00 | 915000.00 |
| More than 8 | 1452679.25 | 850000.00 | 370717.00 | 3740000.00 |

Table 9.2.4 What were the library's total expenditures (in US $) for content/materials in both print and electronic formats in 2019? Broken out by Current operating status of the library

| Current operating status of the library | Mean | Median | Minimum | Maximum |
|---|---|---|---|---|
| We have completely shut the library | 875000.00 | 875000.00 | 875000.00 | 875000.00 |
| We have shut the library to physical traffic but have maintained online access | 730336.93 | 484500.00 | 1000.00 | 3740000.00 |
| We have kept the library open to patrons subject to social distancing and other virus containment measures | 729600.00 | 729600.00 | 92000.00 | 1367200.00 |

Table 9.3.1 What will be the library's total expenditures (in US $) for content/materials in both print and electronic formats in 2020 (anticipated)?

| | Mean | Median | Minimum | Maximum |
|---|---|---|---|---|
| Entire sample | 727224.18 | 500000.00 | 1000.00 | 3740000.00 |

Table 9.3.2 What will be the library's total expenditures (in US $) for content/materials in both print and electronic formats in 2020 (anticipated)? Broken out by Type of law library

| Type of law library | Mean | Median | Minimum | Maximum |
|---|---|---|---|---|
| Law firm library | 534218.50 | 432500.00 | 1000.00 | 1384311.00 |
| University law library | 656125.00 | 725000.00 | 324500.00 | 850000.00 |
| Courthouse library | 542000.00 | 621500.00 | 25000.00 | 900000.00 |
| Non-Courthouse government agency nonprofit or international agency law library | 1455000.00 | 440000.00 | 185000.00 | 3740000.00 |

Table 9.3.3 What will be the library's total expenditures (in US $) for content/materials in both print and electronic formats in 2020 (anticipated)? Broken out by FTE employees

| FTE employees | Mean | Median | Minimum | Maximum |
|---|---|---|---|---|
| Less than 3 | 191666.67 | 185000.00 | 25000.00 | 365000.00 |
| 3 - 4 | 491327.75 | 290000.00 | 1000.00 | 1384311.00 |
| 5 - 8 | 690416.67 | 797500.00 | 324500.00 | 875000.00 |
| More than 8 | 1420000.00 | 750000.00 | 440000.00 | 3740000.00 |

Table 9.3.4 What will be the library's total expenditures (in US $) for content/materials in both print and electronic formats in 2020 (anticipated)? Broken out by Current operating status of the library

| Current operating status of the library | Mean | Median | Minimum | Maximum |
|---|---|---|---|---|
| We have completely shut the library | 850000.00 | 850000.00 | 850000.00 | 850000.00 |
| We have shut the library to physical traffic but have maintained online access | 717750.00 | 499000.00 | 1000.00 | 3740000.00 |
| We have kept the library open to patrons subject to social distancing and other virus containment measures | 732155.50 | 732155.50 | 80000.00 | 1384311.00 |

# Table 10 How much did the library spend (in US $) for online databases in the following years: 2018, 2019 and 2020?

## Table 10.1.1 How much did the library spend (in US $) for online databases in 2018?

| | Mean | Median | Minimum | Maximum |
|---|---|---|---|---|
| Entire sample | 458028.86 | 232500.00 | 17000.00 | 1683799.00 |

## Table 10.1.2 How much did the library spend (in US $) for online databases in 2018? Broken out by Type of law library

| Type of law library | Mean | Median | Minimum | Maximum |
|---|---|---|---|---|
| Law firm library | 601765.40 | 800000.00 | 225000.00 | 900000.00 |
| University law library | 311000.00 | 222000.00 | 200000.00 | 600000.00 |
| Courthouse library | 115666.67 | 160000.00 | 17000.00 | 170000.00 |
| Non-Courthouse government agency nonprofit or international agency law library | 906288.50 | 906288.50 | 128778.00 | 1683799.00 |

## Table 10.1.3 How much did the library spend (in US $) for online databases in 2018? Broken out by FTE employees

| FTE employees | Mean | Median | Minimum | Maximum |
|---|---|---|---|---|
| Less than 3 | 128500.00 | 128500.00 | 17000.00 | 240000.00 |
| 3 - 4 | 656275.67 | 843827.00 | 225000.00 | 900000.00 |
| 5 - 8 | 322800.00 | 200000.00 | 170000.00 | 800000.00 |
| More than 8 | 643144.25 | 380000.00 | 128778.00 | 1683799.00 |

Table 10.1.4 How much did the library spend (in US $) for online databases in 2018? Broken out by Current operating status of the library

| Current operating status of the library | Mean | Median | Minimum | Maximum |
|---|---|---|---|---|
| We have completely shut the library | 200000.00 | 200000.00 | 200000.00 | 200000.00 |
| We have shut the library to physical traffic but have maintained online access | 406234.27 | 225000.00 | 17000.00 | 1683799.00 |
| We have kept the library open to patrons subject to social distancing and other virus containment measures | 871913.50 | 871913.50 | 843827.00 | 900000.00 |

Table 10.2.1 How much did the library spend (in US $) for online databases in 2019?

| | Mean | Median | Minimum | Maximum |
|---|---|---|---|---|
| Entire sample | 522812.79 | 221000.00 | 20000.00 | 1726246.00 |

Table 10.2.2 How much did the library spend (in US $) for online databases in 2019? Broken out by Type of law library

| Type of law library | Mean | Median | Minimum | Maximum |
|---|---|---|---|---|
| Law firm library | 747840.00 | 680000.00 | 200000.00 | 1700000.00 |
| University law library | 335500.00 | 221000.00 | 200000.00 | 700000.00 |
| Courthouse library | 125000.00 | 175000.00 | 20000.00 | 180000.00 |
| Non-Courthouse government agency nonprofit or international agency law library | 931589.50 | 931589.50 | 136933.00 | 1726246.00 |

Table 10.2.3 How much did the library spend (in US $) for online databases in 2019? Broken out by FTE employees

| FTE employees | Mean | Median | Minimum | Maximum |
|---|---|---|---|---|
| Less than 3 | 140000.00 | 140000.00 | 20000.00 | 260000.00 |
| 3 - 4 | 933066.67 | 899200.00 | 200000.00 | 1700000.00 |
| 5 - 8 | 299400.00 | 200000.00 | 175000.00 | 680000.00 |
| More than 8 | 685794.75 | 440000.00 | 136933.00 | 1726246.00 |

### Table 10.2.4 How much did the library spend (in US $) for online databases in 2019? Broken out by Current operating status of the library

| Current operating status of the library | Mean | Median | Minimum | Maximum |
|---|---|---|---|---|
| We have completely shut the library | 200000.00 | 200000.00 | 200000.00 | 200000.00 |
| We have shut the library to physical traffic but have maintained online access | 410925.36 | 200000.00 | 20000.00 | 1726246.00 |
| We have kept the library open to patrons subject to social distancing and other virus containment measures | 1299600.00 | 1299600.00 | 899200.00 | 1700000.00 |

### Table 10.3.1 How much will the library spend (in US $) for online databases in 2020 (anticipated)?

| | Mean | Median | Minimum | Maximum |
|---|---|---|---|---|
| Entire sample | 518556.86 | 218000.00 | 15000.00 | 2000000.00 |

Table 10.3.2 How much will the library spend (in US $) for online databases in 2020 (anticipated)? Broken out by Type of law library

| Type of law library | Mean | Median | Minimum | Maximum |
|---|---|---|---|---|
| Law firm library | 683959.20 | 500000.00 | 175000.00 | 1700000.00 |
| University law library | 311250.00 | 247500.00 | 200000.00 | 550000.00 |
| Courthouse library | 131666.67 | 180000.00 | 15000.00 | 200000.00 |
| Non-Courthouse government agency nonprofit or international agency law library | 1100000.00 | 1100000.00 | 200000.00 | 2000000.00 |

Table 10.3.3 How much will the library spend (in US $) for online databases in 2020 (anticipated)? Broken out by FTE employees

| FTE employees | Mean | Median | Minimum | Maximum |
|---|---|---|---|---|
| Less than 3 | 125500.00 | 125500.00 | 15000.00 | 236000.00 |
| 3 - 4 | 894598.67 | 808796.00 | 175000.00 | 1700000.00 |
| 5 - 8 | 275000.00 | 200000.00 | 180000.00 | 500000.00 |
| More than 8 | 737500.00 | 375000.00 | 200000.00 | 2000000.00 |

Table 10.3.4 How much will the library spend (in US $) for online databases in 2020 (anticipated)? Broken out by Current operating status of the library

| Current operating status of the library | Mean | Median | Minimum | Maximum |
|---|---|---|---|---|
| We have completely shut the library | 200000.00 | 200000.00 | 200000.00 | 200000.00 |
| We have shut the library to physical traffic but have maintained online access | 413727.27 | 200000.00 | 15000.00 | 2000000.00 |
| We have kept the library open to patrons subject to social distancing and other virus containment measures | 1254398.00 | 1254398.00 | 808796.00 | 1700000.00 |

## Table 11 Over the next year do you feel that your law library will spend more, spend less, spend about the same, or continue not to use the following suppliers of legal information?

### Table 11.1.1 Over the next year do you feel that your law library will spend more, spend less, spend about the same, or continue not to use the Bloomberg?

| | No Answer | Spend More | Spend About the Same | Spend Less | Continue not to Use |
|---|---|---|---|---|---|
| Entire sample | 2.86% | 0.00% | 57.14% | 14.29% | 25.71% |

### Table 11.1.2 Over the next year do you feel that your law library will spend more, spend less, spend about the same, or continue not to use the Bloomberg? Broken out by Type of law library

| Type of law library | No Answer | Spend More | Spend About the Same | Spend Less | Continue not to Use |
|---|---|---|---|---|---|
| Law firm library | 0.00% | 0.00% | 60.00% | 13.33% | 26.67% |
| University law library | 10.00% | 0.00% | 90.00% | 0.00% | 0.00% |
| Courthouse library | 0.00% | 0.00% | 28.57% | 28.57% | 42.86% |
| Non-Courthouse government agency nonprofit or international agency law library | 0.00% | 0.00% | 0.00% | 33.33% | 66.67% |

Table 11.1.3 Over the next year do you feel that your law library will spend more, spend less, spend about the same, or continue not to use the Bloomberg? Broken out by FTE employees

| FTE employees | No Answer | Spend More | Spend About the Same | Spend Less | Continue not to Use |
|---|---|---|---|---|---|
| Less than 3 | 0.00% | 0.00% | 50.00% | 12.50% | 37.50% |
| 3 - 4 | 0.00% | 0.00% | 55.56% | 11.11% | 33.33% |
| 5 - 8 | 10.00% | 0.00% | 70.00% | 10.00% | 10.00% |
| More than 8 | 0.00% | 0.00% | 50.00% | 25.00% | 25.00% |

Table 11.1.4 Over the next year do you feel that your law library will spend more, spend less, spend about the same, or continue not to use the Bloomberg? Broken out by Current operating status of the library

| Current operating status of the library | No Answer | Spend More | Spend About the Same | Spend Less | Continue not to Use |
|---|---|---|---|---|---|
| We have completely shut the library | 100.00% | 0.00% | 0.00% | 0.00% | 0.00% |
| We have shut the library to physical traffic but have maintained online access | 0.00% | 0.00% | 59.26% | 14.81% | 25.93% |
| We have kept the library open to patrons subject to social distancing and other virus containment measures | 0.00% | 0.00% | 100.00% | 0.00% | 0.00% |
| We have not really made any major changes in terms of patron access | 0.00% | 0.00% | 0.00% | 33.33% | 66.67% |

Table 11.2.1 Over the next year do you feel that your law library will spend more, spend less, spend about the same, or continue not to use the Thomson/Reuters/West?

| | No Answer | Spend More | Spend About the Same | Spend Less | Continue not to Use |
|---|---|---|---|---|---|
| Entire sample | 0.00% | 5.71% | 71.43% | 20.00% | 2.86% |

Table 11.2.2 Over the next year do you feel that your law library will spend more, spend less, spend about the same, or continue not to use the Thomson/Reuters/West? Broken out by Type of law library

| Type of law library | No Answer | Spend More | Spend About the Same | Spend Less | Continue not to Use |
|---|---|---|---|---|---|
| Law firm library | 0.00% | 0.00% | 73.33% | 20.00% | 6.67% |
| University law library | 0.00% | 0.00% | 90.00% | 10.00% | 0.00% |
| Courthouse library | 0.00% | 0.00% | 57.14% | 42.86% | 0.00% |
| Non-Courthouse government agency nonprofit or international agency law library | 0.00% | 66.67% | 33.33% | 0.00% | 0.00% |

Table 11.2.3 Over the next year do you feel that your law library will spend more, spend less, spend about the same, or continue not to use the Thomson/Reuters/West? Broken out by FTE employees

| FTE employees | No Answer | Spend More | Spend About the Same | Spend Less | Continue not to Use |
|---|---|---|---|---|---|
| Less than 3 | 0.00% | 12.50% | 75.00% | 12.50% | 0.00% |
| 3 - 4 | 0.00% | 0.00% | 66.67% | 22.22% | 11.11% |
| 5 - 8 | 0.00% | 0.00% | 70.00% | 30.00% | 0.00% |
| More than 8 | 0.00% | 12.50% | 75.00% | 12.50% | 0.00% |

Table 11.2.4 Over the next year do you feel that your law library will spend more, spend less, spend about the same, or continue not to use the Thomson/Reuters/West? Broken out by Current operating status of the library

| Current operating status of the library | No Answer | Spend More | Spend About the Same | Spend Less | Continue not to Use |
|---|---|---|---|---|---|
| We have completely shut the library | 0.00% | 0.00% | 100.00% | 0.00% | 0.00% |
| We have shut the library to physical traffic but have maintained online access | 0.00% | 7.41% | 70.37% | 18.52% | 3.70% |
| We have kept the library open to patrons subject to social distancing and other virus containment measures | 0.00% | 0.00% | 75.00% | 25.00% | 0.00% |
| We have not really made any major changes in terms of patron access | 0.00% | 0.00% | 66.67% | 33.33% | 0.00% |

Table 11.3.1 Over the next year do you feel that your law library will spend more, spend less, spend about the same, or continue not to use the Reed/Elsevier/LexisNexis?

| | No Answer | Spend More | Spend About the Same | Spend Less | Continue not to Use |
|---|---|---|---|---|---|
| Entire sample | 0.00% | 2.86% | 65.71% | 17.14% | 14.29% |

Table 11.3.2 Over the next year do you feel that your law library will spend more, spend less, spend about the same, or continue not to use the Reed/Elsevier/LexisNexis? Broken out by Type of law library

| Type of law library | No Answer | Spend More | Spend About the Same | Spend Less | Continue not to Use |
|---|---|---|---|---|---|
| Law firm library | 0.00% | 6.67% | 46.67% | 20.00% | 26.67% |
| University law library | 0.00% | 0.00% | 80.00% | 20.00% | 0.00% |
| Courthouse library | 0.00% | 0.00% | 71.43% | 14.29% | 14.29% |
| Non-Courthouse government agency nonprofit or international agency law library | 0.00% | 0.00% | 100.00% | 0.00% | 0.00% |

Table 11.3.3 Over the next year do you feel that your law library will spend more, spend less, spend about the same, or continue not to use the Reed/Elsevier/LexisNexis? Broken out by FTE employees

| FTE employees | No Answer | Spend More | Spend About the Same | Spend Less | Continue not to Use |
|---|---|---|---|---|---|
| Less than 3 | 0.00% | 12.50% | 62.50% | 0.00% | 25.00% |
| 3 - 4 | 0.00% | 0.00% | 55.56% | 22.22% | 22.22% |
| 5 - 8 | 0.00% | 0.00% | 70.00% | 20.00% | 10.00% |
| More than 8 | 0.00% | 0.00% | 75.00% | 25.00% | 0.00% |

Table 11.3.4 Over the next year do you feel that your law library will spend more, spend less, spend about the same, or continue not to use the Reed/Elsevier/LexisNexis? Broken out by Current operating status of the library

| Current operating status of the library | No Answer | Spend More | Spend About the Same | Spend Less | Continue not to Use |
|---|---|---|---|---|---|
| We have completely shut the library | 0.00% | 0.00% | 100.00% | 0.00% | 0.00% |
| We have shut the library to physical traffic but have maintained online access | 0.00% | 0.00% | 70.37% | 18.52% | 11.11% |
| We have kept the library open to patrons subject to social distancing and other virus containment measures | 0.00% | 25.00% | 25.00% | 0.00% | 50.00% |
| We have not really made any major changes in terms of patron access | 0.00% | 0.00% | 66.67% | 33.33% | 0.00% |

Table 11.4.1 Over the next year do you feel that your law library will spend more, spend less, spend about the same, or continue not to use the Wolters/Kluwers/CHH?

| | No Answer | Spend More | Spend About the Same | Spend Less | Continue not to Use |
|---|---|---|---|---|---|
| Entire sample | 0.00% | 2.86% | 48.57% | 37.14% | 11.43% |

Table 11.4.2 Over the next year do you feel that your law library will spend more, spend less, spend about the same, or continue not to use the Wolters/Kluwers/CHH? Broken out by Type of law library

| Type of law library | No Answer | Spend More | Spend About the Same | Spend Less | Continue not to Use |
|---|---|---|---|---|---|
| Law firm library | 0.00% | 6.67% | 40.00% | 46.67% | 6.67% |
| University law library | 0.00% | 0.00% | 70.00% | 20.00% | 10.00% |
| Courthouse library | 0.00% | 0.00% | 28.57% | 42.86% | 28.57% |
| Non-Courthouse government agency nonprofit or international agency law library | 0.00% | 0.00% | 66.67% | 33.33% | 0.00% |

Table 11.4.3 Over the next year do you feel that your law library will spend more, spend less, spend about the same, or continue not to use the Wolters/Kluwers/CHH? Broken out by FTE employees

| FTE employees | No Answer | Spend More | Spend About the Same | Spend Less | Continue not to Use |
|---|---|---|---|---|---|
| Less than 3 | 0.00% | 12.50% | 37.50% | 37.50% | 12.50% |
| 3 - 4 | 0.00% | 0.00% | 44.44% | 55.56% | 0.00% |
| 5 - 8 | 0.00% | 0.00% | 70.00% | 10.00% | 20.00% |
| More than 8 | 0.00% | 0.00% | 37.50% | 50.00% | 12.50% |

Table 11.4.4 Over the next year do you feel that your law library will spend more, spend less, spend about the same, or continue not to use the Wolters/Kluwers/CHH? Broken out by Current operating status of the library

| Current operating status of the library | No Answer | Spend More | Spend About the Same | Spend Less | Continue not to Use |
|---|---|---|---|---|---|
| We have completely shut the library | 0.00% | 0.00% | 100.00% | 0.00% | 0.00% |
| We have shut the library to physical traffic but have maintained online access | 0.00% | 0.00% | 48.15% | 37.04% | 14.81% |
| We have kept the library open to patrons subject to social distancing and other virus containment measures | 0.00% | 0.00% | 25.00% | 75.00% | 0.00% |
| We have not really made any major changes in terms of patron access | 0.00% | 33.33% | 66.67% | 0.00% | 0.00% |

Table 11.5.1 Over the next year do you feel that your law library will spend more, spend less, spend about the same, or continue not to use the American Bar Association?

| | No Answer | Spend More | Spend About the Same | Spend Less | Continue not to Use |
|---|---|---|---|---|---|
| Entire sample | 2.86% | 0.00% | 42.86% | 20.00% | 34.29% |

Table 11.5.2 Over the next year do you feel that your law library will spend more, spend less, spend about the same, or continue not to use the American Bar Association? Broken out by Type of law library

| Type of law library | No Answer | Spend More | Spend About the Same | Spend Less | Continue not to Use |
|---|---|---|---|---|---|
| Law firm library | 0.00% | 0.00% | 26.67% | 6.67% | 66.67% |
| University law library | 0.00% | 0.00% | 80.00% | 10.00% | 10.00% |
| Courthouse library | 14.29% | 0.00% | 14.29% | 57.14% | 14.29% |
| Non-Courthouse government agency nonprofit or international agency law library | 0.00% | 0.00% | 66.67% | 33.33% | 0.00% |

Table 11.5.3 Over the next year do you feel that your law library will spend more, spend less, spend about the same, or continue not to use the American Bar Association? Broken out by FTE employees

| FTE employees | No Answer | Spend More | Spend About the Same | Spend Less | Continue not to Use |
|---|---|---|---|---|---|
| Less than 3 | 0.00% | 0.00% | 25.00% | 12.50% | 62.50% |
| 3 - 4 | 0.00% | 0.00% | 22.22% | 33.33% | 44.44% |
| 5 - 8 | 0.00% | 0.00% | 60.00% | 10.00% | 30.00% |
| More than 8 | 12.50% | 0.00% | 62.50% | 25.00% | 0.00% |

Table 11.5.4 Over the next year do you feel that your law library will spend more, spend less, spend about the same, or continue not to use the American Bar Association? Broken out by Current operating status of the library

| Current operating status of the library | No Answer | Spend More | Spend About the Same | Spend Less | Continue not to Use |
|---|---|---|---|---|---|
| We have completely shut the library | 0.00% | 0.00% | 100.00% | 0.00% | 0.00% |
| We have shut the library to physical traffic but have maintained online access | 3.70% | 0.00% | 44.44% | 22.22% | 29.63% |
| We have kept the library open to patrons subject to social distancing and other virus containment measures | 0.00% | 0.00% | 50.00% | 25.00% | 25.00% |
| We have not really made any major changes in terms of patron access | 0.00% | 0.00% | 0.00% | 0.00% | 100.00% |

## Table 12.1 Which of the following do you feel has most reached out to help during the coronavirus epidemic?

| | Other | LexisNexis | West/Thomson-Reuters | Bloomberg | Hein | FastCase | Google Scholar |
|---|---|---|---|---|---|---|---|
| Entire sample | 25.71% | 31.43% | 34.29% | 0.00% | 5.71% | 2.86% | 0.00% |

## Table 12.2 Which of the following do you feel has most reached out to help during the coronavirus epidemic? Broken out by Type of law library

| Type of law library | Other | LexisNexis | West/Thomson-Reuters | Bloomberg | Hein | FastCase | Google Scholar |
|---|---|---|---|---|---|---|---|
| Law firm library | 26.67% | 33.33% | 26.67% | 0.00% | 6.67% | 6.67% | 0.00% |
| University law library | 40.00% | 20.00% | 30.00% | 0.00% | 10.00% | 0.00% | 0.00% |
| Courthouse library | 14.29% | 42.86% | 42.86% | 0.00% | 0.00% | 0.00% | 0.00% |
| Non-Courthouse government agency nonprofit or international agency law library | 0.00% | 33.33% | 66.67% | 0.00% | 0.00% | 0.00% | 0.00% |

## Table 12.3 Which of the following do you feel has most reached out to help during the coronavirus epidemic? Broken out by FTE employees

| FTE employees | Other | LexisNexis | West/Thomson-Reuters | Bloomberg | Hein | FastCase | Google Scholar |
|---|---|---|---|---|---|---|---|
| Less than 3 | 25.00% | 25.00% | 50.00% | 0.00% | 0.00% | 0.00% | 0.00% |
| 3 - 4 | 22.22% | 33.33% | 33.33% | 0.00% | 11.11% | 0.00% | 0.00% |
| 5 - 8 | 40.00% | 30.00% | 30.00% | 0.00% | 0.00% | 0.00% | 0.00% |
| More than 8 | 12.50% | 37.50% | 25.00% | 0.00% | 12.50% | 12.50% | 0.00% |

## Table 12.4 Which of the following do you feel has most reached out to help during the coronavirus epidemic? Broken out by Current operating status of the library

| Current operating status of the library | Other | LexisNexis | West/Thomson-Reuters | Bloomberg | Hein | FastCase | Google Scholar |
|---|---|---|---|---|---|---|---|
| We have completely shut the library | 0.00% | 0.00% | 100.00% | 0.00% | 0.00 % | 0.00 % | 0.00 % |
| We have shut the library to physical traffic but have maintained online access | 25.93 % | 29.63% | 33.33% | 0.00% | 7.41 % | 3.70 % | 0.00 % |
| We have kept the library open to patrons subject to social distancing and other virus containment measures | 50.00 % | 0.00% | 50.00% | 0.00% | 0.00 % | 0.00 % | 0.00 % |
| We have not really made any major changes in terms of patron access | 0.00% | 100.00 % | 0.00% | 0.00% | 0.00 % | 0.00 % | 0.00 % |

Other:

1. CEB
2. No one, really.
3. none - they all are trying to stay afloat as well
4. All vendors that we have reached out to have been helpful, but few initiated useful contact with us first.
5. Wolters Kluwer
6. None - we reached out to THEM
7. n/a
8. All but Google Vendors have been very good at reaching out Include PLI in that too
9. Outreach has been the same among LN, WL, Hein. I have had limited outreach from Bloomberg and none from FastCase or Google Scholar.

## Table 13.1 How important do you feel it is to acquaint your library's end users with newly emerging automated and robotic methods of conducting legal information searches?

| | No Answer | Absolutely critical as it is the wave of the future | Very important right now | Important but not a big factor right now | Useful perhaps but still more theoretical than actual | Hyped a bit too much, not really a factor now | Have not really heard about it and not asked about it at all |
|---|---|---|---|---|---|---|---|
| Entire sample | 5.71% | 22.86% | 22.86% | 31.43% | 8.57% | 0.00% | 8.57% |

## Table 13.2 How important do you feel it is to acquaint your library's end users with newly emerging automated and robotic methods of conducting legal information searches? Broken out by Type of law library

| Type of law library | No Answer | Absolutely critical as it is the wave of the future | Very important right now | Important but not a big factor right now | Useful perhaps but still more theoretical than actual | Hyped a bit too much, not really a factor now | Have not really heard about it and not asked about it at all |
|---|---|---|---|---|---|---|---|
| Law firm library | 6.67% | 33.33% | 6.67% | 33.33% | 13.33% | 0.00% | 6.67% |
| University law library | 10.00% | 20.00% | 20.00% | 30.00% | 10.00% | 0.00% | 10.00% |
| Courthouse library | 0.00% | 14.29% | 42.86% | 28.57% | 0.00% | 0.00% | 14.29% |
| Non-Courthouse government agency nonprofit or international agency law library | 0.00% | 0.00% | 66.67% | 33.33% | 0.00% | 0.00% | 0.00% |

## Table 13.3 How important do you feel it is to acquaint your library's end users with newly emerging automated and robotic methods of conducting legal information searches? Broken out by FTE employees

| FTE employees | No Answer | Absolutely critical as it is the wave of the future | Very important right now | Important but not a big factor right now | Useful perhaps but still more theoretical than actual | Hyped a bit too much, not really a factor now | Have not really heard about it and not asked about it at all |
|---|---|---|---|---|---|---|---|
| Less than 3 | 0.00% | 37.50% | 12.50% | 25.00% | 12.50% | 0.00% | 12.50% |
| 3 - 4 | 0.00% | 0.00% | 11.11% | 66.67% | 11.11% | 0.00% | 11.11% |
| 5 - 8 | 10.00% | 20.00% | 40.00% | 20.00% | 0.00% | 0.00% | 10.00% |
| More than 8 | 12.50% | 37.50% | 25.00% | 12.50% | 12.50% | 0.00% | 0.00% |

## Table 13.4 How important do you feel it is to acquaint your library's end users with newly emerging automated and robotic methods of conducting legal information searches? Broken out by Current operating status of the library

| Current operating status of the library | No Answer | Absolutely critical as it is the wave of the future | Very important right now | Important but not a big factor right now | Useful perhaps but still more theoretical than actual | Hyped a bit too much, not really a factor now | Have not really heard about it and not asked about it at all |
|---|---|---|---|---|---|---|---|
| We have completely shut the library | 0.00% | 0.00% | 100.00% | 0.00% | 0.00% | 0.00% | 0.00% |
| We have shut the library to physical traffic but have maintained online access | 7.41% | 25.93% | 22.22% | 29.63% | 7.41% | 0.00% | 7.41% |
| We have kept the library open to patrons subject to social distancing and other virus containment measures | 0.00% | 0.00% | 25.00% | 50.00% | 0.00% | 0.00% | 25.00% |
| We have not really made any major changes in terms of patron access | 0.00% | 33.33% | 0.00% | 33.33% | 33.33% | 0.00% | 0.00% |

## What steps has your library taken to familiarize your organization's librarians with artificial intelligence approaches to legal information searching? Broken out by Type of law library

Law firm library

1) On-line seminar attendance, publications
2) None
3) Nothing as of yet.
4) A few demos, but what we have seen so far has been underwhelming.
5) conferences
6) Just learning about what's out there and looking at it. We are moving that way
7) We use some AI resources now and meet with vendors/trainers regularly to keep on top of evolving technology and resources.
8) more webinars and constant monitoring
9) I stay up-to-date via ILTA, AALL, SLA, and vendor webinars and conferences.
10) Encourage & promote online learning opportunities through vendor and professional association webinars
11) We have provided training for online services which provide analytics.
12) none

University law library

1) Online seminars
2) Online training and news updates.
3) Promote educational opportunities to the librarians.
4) Teaching.
5) Webinars
6) Attending conferences, webinars, and reading studies
7) None - they get that information in their Legal Research classes
8) Vendor demos

Courthouse library

1) None.
2) Does not apply
3) AI is not a big issue or topic of interest in the court setting, in terms of acquiring/implementing AI solutions.
4) none
5) We've attended seminars provided by Lexis and Westlaw as well as Bloomberg/BNA.

6) As director I have made sure that my librarians know about AI generally as well as which tools, we already have with AI features. AI is a pet project of mine, so I definitely talk about it a lot with my staff.

Non-Courthouse government agency nonprofit or international agency law library

1) We have purchased continuing education book Law Librarianship in the Age of AI and encourage online learning in this area.
2) Very little at the moment
3) Still in planning stages

## Which law artificial intelligence products have been, or you think will be, most useful for your organization? Why? Broken out by Type of law library

Law firm library

1) The built in analytics in Westlaw's newest version are extremely helpful as is LawGeex, Ross Intelligence
2) None
3) Anything really, really good for legislative monitoring. None are at that stage for the present.
4) none at this time.
5) WESTLAWEDGE
6) Many departments are checking out analytics materials like Lex Machina and Westlaw Edge. These products can save attorneys time and hopefully impress prospective clients.
7) n/a
8) brief analysis tools, brief drafting tools, contract review tools, contracting drafting tools, AI-enhanced legal research, jurisdictional surveys on-demand
9) Westlaw litigation analytics & Lexis Context; in the future very interested in Fastcase AI sandbox
10) Westlaw Analytics and Bloomberg Law. These are the ones we currently subscribe to. We are not looking to pay for any new services at this time.
11) none

University law library

1) Westlaw, Lexis, Ross
2) Ross, and court analytics. We have a strong bankruptcy program which Ross will aid. Our faculty does interdisciplinary research so court analytics will be useful for them, and for student jobseekers.
3) Legal databases.
4) The databases
5) AI is built into just about every major search platform these days, so our librarians are quite familiar with those. Data mining and competitive analytic products will increase in use over time (and just continues a trend we saw long before the pandemic)
6) there is not a preference our students mostly use it to do their homework before job interviews
7) none/unknown
8) None

Courthouse library

1) None.
2) None
3) Nothing comes to mind that I am aware of.
4) none
5) All of the above databases.
6) Westlaw Edge's Brief Check and the comparable feature on CaseText's CARA. Working for a court, I think our staff attorneys and law clerks could benefit from an AI tool to double-check their own research to uncover authority beyond what is cited by the parties.

Non-Courthouse government agency nonprofit or international agency law library

1) Chatbots possibly; form-filling guidance products.
2) Our organization is still gathering information on the subject, mainly by reviewing recent articles and books.
3) Unsure at present

## Table 14.1 How influential would you say that the law library is relative to the norm for other departments and agencies within your organization -- in its ability to protect its interests, particularly in budget negotiations?

| | No Answer | The Library is More Influential than the Norm for other Players | The Library is About as Influential as the Norm for other Players | The Library is Less Influential than the Norm for other Players |
|---|---|---|---|---|
| Entire sample | 11.43% | 14.29% | 62.86% | 11.43% |

## Table 14.2 How influential would you say that the law library is relative to the norm for other departments and agencies within your organization -- in its ability to protect its interests, particularly in budget negotiations? Broken out by Type of law library

| Type of law library | No Answer | The Library is More Influential than the Norm for other Players | The Library is About as Influential as the Norm for other Players | The Library is Less Influential than the Norm for other Players |
|---|---|---|---|---|
| Law firm library | 6.67% | 13.33% | 66.67% | 13.33% |
| University law library | 20.00% | 20.00% | 60.00% | 0.00% |
| Courthouse library | 14.29% | 14.29% | 42.86% | 28.57% |
| Non-Courthouse government agency nonprofit or international agency law library | 0.00% | 0.00% | 100.00% | 0.00% |

## Table 14.3 How influential would you say that the law library is relative to the norm for other departments and agencies within your organization -- in its ability to protect its interests, particularly in budget negotiations? Broken out by FTE employees

| FTE employees | No Answer | The Library is More Influential than the Norm for other Players | The Library is About as Influential as the Norm for other Players | The Library is Less Influential than the Norm for other Players |
|---|---|---|---|---|
| Less than 3 | 12.50% | 0.00% | 75.00% | 12.50% |
| 3 - 4 | 0.00% | 22.22% | 66.67% | 11.11% |
| 5 - 8 | 20.00% | 10.00% | 60.00% | 10.00% |
| More than 8 | 12.50% | 25.00% | 50.00% | 12.50% |

## Table 14.4 How influential would you say that the law library is relative to the norm for other departments and agencies within your organization -- in its ability to protect its interests, particularly in budget negotiations? Broken out by Current operating status of the library

| Current operating status of the library | No Answer | The Library is More Influential than the Norm for other Players | The Library is About as Influential as the Norm for other Players | The Library is Less Influential than the Norm for other Players |
|---|---|---|---|---|
| We have completely shut the library | 0.00% | 100.00% | 0.00% | 0.00% |
| We have shut the library to physical traffic but have maintained online access | 14.81% | 11.11% | 62.96% | 11.11% |
| We have kept the library open to patrons subject to social distancing and other virus containment measures | 0.00% | 25.00% | 75.00% | 0.00% |
| We have not really made any major changes in terms of patron access | 0.00% | 0.00% | 66.67% | 33.33% |

## What tools does the library use to monitor how much various library databases, software and other tools are used by its patrons? Broken out by Type of law library

Law firm library

1) Internal monitoring of providers usage data and bar code check out
2) Vendor statistics
3) Nothing except the tools offered by the vendors for their respective products.
4) Vendor reporting metrics.
5) none
6) I only check WESTLAW usage
7) I regularly retrieve (e.g. Quickview, Westlaw Analytics) or request usage reports from IT or our vendors for our main online resources. I also contact attorneys directly on the value of certain products.
8) the monthly billing
9) Onelog Electronic Resource Management (ERM) software
10) Research Monitor; vendor usage files
11) We do not currently monitor this usage. I would be interested is finding out what other librarians are using.
12) Usage tracking tools that come with the databases
13) n/a

University law library

1) Vendor statistics if available, student surveys, focus groups
2) Usage statistics, checkout statistics, student and faculty surveys, and anecdotal feedback.
3) Usage statistics.
4) ERM.
5) Various. (We get usage reports from both vendors and our proxy server)
6) google analytics, click-through tracking, proxy access, and vendor usage stats
7) Good old fashioned eyeballing of circulation data. Please note that databases are notorious for providing terrible stats data though.
8) COUNTER; LibGuides Stats

Courthouse library

1) None.
2) Knowledge Tracker, Invoices, Tracking Reports from Vendors
3) Vendor-supplied tools or resources.
4) Hand count by staff. Electronic usage tabulated by Westlaw for each terminal location.
5) We don't monitor the databases the patrons use. We have an overall idea which databases are used since Westlaw and Lexis are on separate computers.
6) we rely primarily on vendor-supplied usage statistics
7) Usage statistics

Non-Courthouse government agency nonprofit or international agency law library

1) We detail usage reports on an annual basis. We teach classes on databases and monitor usage increases.
2) Usage statistics provided by publishers/vendors and library-generated questionnaires and surveys.
3) Direct reports from vendors

## Table 15.1 About how often do you present library tool usage data to organization executives outside of the law library? (i.e., law partners/management committee, university deans, government agency management, etc.)

| | No Answer | Monthly or More Frequently | Every few months | Every 6 months or so | Annually | Once every few years | More or Less Never |
|---|---|---|---|---|---|---|---|
| Entire sample | 8.57% | 17.14% | 8.57% | 5.71% | 31.43% | 5.71 % | 22.86 % |

## Table 15.2 About how often do you present library tool usage data to organization executives outside of the law library? (i.e., law partners/management committee, university deans, government agency management, etc.) Broken out by Type of law library

| Type of law library | No Answer | Monthly or More Frequently | Every few months | Every 6 months or so | Annually | Once every few years | More or Less Never |
|---|---|---|---|---|---|---|---|
| Law firm library | 6.67% | 20.00% | 6.67% | 0.00% | 20.00% | 13.33 % | 33.33 % |
| University law library | 20.00 % | 10.00% | 10.00 % | 0.00% | 50.00% | 0.00% | 10.00 % |
| Courthouse library | 0.00% | 14.29% | 14.29 % | 0.00% | 42.86% | 0.00% | 28.57 % |
| Non-Courthouse government agency nonprofit or international agency law library | 0.00% | 33.33% | 0.00% | 66.67 % | 0.00% | 0.00% | 0.00% |

## Table 15.3 About how often do you present library tool usage data to organization executives outside of the law library? (i.e., law partners/management committee, university deans, government agency management, etc.) Broken out by FTE employees

| FTE employees | No Answer | Monthly or More Frequently | Every few months | Every 6 months or so | Annually | Once every few years | More or Less Never |
|---|---|---|---|---|---|---|---|
| Less than 3 | 0.00% | 0.00% | 0.00% | 12.50 % | 12.50% | 25.00 % | 50.00 % |
| 3 - 4 | 0.00% | 33.33% | 11.11 % | 0.00% | 44.44% | 0.00% | 11.11 % |
| 5 - 8 | 20.00 % | 10.00% | 10.00 % | 0.00% | 40.00% | 0.00% | 20.00 % |
| More than 8 | 12.50 % | 25.00% | 12.50 % | 12.50 % | 25.00% | 0.00% | 12.50 % |

## Table 15.4 About how often do you present library tool usage data to organization executives outside of the law library? (i.e., law partners/management committee, university deans, government agency management, etc.) Broken out by Current operating status of the library

| Current operating status of the library | No Answer | Monthly or More Frequently | Every few months | Every 6 months or so | Annually | Once every few years | More or Less Never |
|---|---|---|---|---|---|---|---|
| We have completely shut the library | 0.00% | 0.00% | 0.00% | 0.00% | 100.00% | 0.00% | 0.00% |
| We have shut the library to physical traffic but have maintained online access | 11.11% | 14.81% | 11.11% | 7.41% | 33.33% | 0.00% | 22.22% |
| We have kept the library open to patrons subject to social distancing and other virus containment measures | 0.00% | 50.00% | 0.00% | 0.00% | 0.00% | 25.00% | 25.00% |
| We have not really made any major changes in terms of patron access | 0.00% | 0.00% | 0.00% | 0.00% | 33.33% | 33.33% | 33.33% |

## What kind of help has your library received from your consortium in dealing with the impact of the coronavirus epidemic on the library? Broken out by Type of law library

Law firm library

1) None
2) Not member of a consortium
3) N/A
4) The state-wide group of County Law Library Directors has been having every other week conference calls/zoom meetings.
5) I receive email & newsletters and webinar information
6) No consortium. Other than the furloughed library staff and certain print products not being processed working remotely has not affected our ability to do our jobs. The vendors have even been cooperative in providing online access for the few print products we have.
7) status quo -
8) na
9) NA
10) None at this time.
11) No consortium, but very supportive informal network of librarians.
12) none

University law library

1) NELLCO has added new products, like Leopard, that will help us reduce costs.
2) Carli -- continued to move forward with implementation of Alma.
3) One consortium has actually increased database options. Another consortium has discontinued shared print collection.
4) Increased scanning services; coordinated loan extensions
5) none/unknown
6) NA

Courthouse library

1) None.
2) None
3) None to date.
4) encouragement
5) There has been minimal interaction at the individual law library level.
6) we do not belong to a consortium
7) Weekly meetings and discussion, sharing of information and knowledge regarding operations and potential re-opening.

Non-Courthouse government agency nonprofit or international agency law library

1) There has been some CRIV support with vendor negotiation of remote access to databases for our users and also in stopping shipments and holding invoices during our closure.
2) N/A
3) This question is too vaguely worded to be answered meaningfully.

## Table 16 How many subscriptions that require payment does the library maintain to legal journals in the following formats:

### Table 16.1.1 How many subscriptions that require payment does the library maintain to legal journals in print with no electronic access format?

| | Mean | Median | Minimum | Maximum |
|---|---|---|---|---|
| Entire sample | 26.94 | 10.00 | 0.00 | 196.00 |

### Table 16.1.2 How many subscriptions that require payment does the library maintain to legal journals in print with no electronic access format? Broken out by Type of law library

| Type of law library | Mean | Median | Minimum | Maximum |
|---|---|---|---|---|
| Law firm library | 48.71 | 15.00 | 0.00 | 196.00 |
| University law library | 15.00 | 15.00 | 3.00 | 27.00 |
| Courthouse library | 3.33 | 0.00 | 0.00 | 10.00 |
| Non-Courthouse government agency nonprofit or international agency law library | 10.00 | 10.00 | 10.00 | 10.00 |

### Table 16.1.3 How many subscriptions that require payment does the library maintain to legal journals in print with no electronic access format? Broken out by FTE employees

| FTE employees | Mean | Median | Minimum | Maximum |
|---|---|---|---|---|
| Less than 3 | 41.67 | 60.00 | 0.00 | 65.00 |
| 3 - 4 | 52.75 | 7.50 | 0.00 | 196.00 |
| 5 - 8 | 12.40 | 15.00 | 0.00 | 27.00 |
| More than 8 | 8.25 | 10.00 | 3.00 | 10.00 |

Table 16.1.4 How many subscriptions that require payment does the library maintain to legal journals in print with no electronic access format? Broken out by Current operating status of the library

| Current operating status of the library | Mean | Median | Minimum | Maximum |
|---|---|---|---|---|
| We have completely shut the library | 15.00 | 15.00 | 15.00 | 15.00 |
| We have shut the library to physical traffic but have maintained online access | 12.92 | 10.00 | 0.00 | 60.00 |
| We have kept the library open to patrons subject to social distancing and other virus containment measures | 98.00 | 98.00 | 0.00 | 196.00 |
| We have not really made any major changes in terms of patron access | 65.00 | 65.00 | 65.00 | 65.00 |

Table 16.2.1 How many subscriptions that require payment does the library maintain to legal journals in electronic with no print counterpart format?

| | Mean | Median | Minimum | Maximum |
|---|---|---|---|---|
| Entire sample | 57.55 | 10.00 | 2.00 | 220.00 |

### Table 16.2.2 How many subscriptions that require payment does the library maintain to legal journals in electronic with no print counterpart format? Broken out by Type of law library

| Type of law library | Mean | Median | Minimum | Maximum |
|---|---|---|---|---|
| Law firm library | 35.00 | 17.50 | 5.00 | 100.00 |
| University law library | 118.75 | 126.50 | 2.00 | 220.00 |
| Courthouse library | 5.00 | 5.00 | 5.00 | 5.00 |
| Non-Courthouse government agency nonprofit or international agency law library | 6.50 | 6.50 | 3.00 | 10.00 |

### Table 16.2.3 How many subscriptions that require payment does the library maintain to legal journals in electronic with no print counterpart format? Broken out by FTE employees

| FTE employees | Mean | Median | Minimum | Maximum |
|---|---|---|---|---|
| Less than 3 | 15.00 | 15.00 | 5.00 | 25.00 |
| 3 - 4 | 100.00 | 100.00 | 100.00 | 100.00 |
| 5 - 8 | 120.75 | 126.50 | 10.00 | 220.00 |
| More than 8 | 5.00 | 4.00 | 2.00 | 10.00 |

Table 16.2.4 How many subscriptions that require payment does the library maintain to legal journals in electronic with no print counterpart format? Broken out by Current operating status of the library

| Current operating status of the library | Mean | Median | Minimum | Maximum |
|---|---|---|---|---|
| We have completely shut the library | 220.00 | 220.00 | 220.00 | 220.00 |
| We have shut the library to physical traffic but have maintained online access | 45.33 | 10.00 | 2.00 | 220.00 |
| We have not really made any major changes in terms of patron access | 5.00 | 5.00 | 5.00 | 5.00 |

Table 16.3.1 How many subscriptions that require payment does the library maintain to legal journals in both print and electronic access format?

| | Mean | Median | Minimum | Maximum |
|---|---|---|---|---|
| Entire sample | 17.71 | 10.00 | 1.00 | 90.00 |

Table 16.3.2 How many subscriptions that require payment does the library maintain to legal journals in both print and electronic access format? Broken out by Type of law library

| Type of law library | Mean | Median | Minimum | Maximum |
|---|---|---|---|---|
| Law firm library | 15.00 | 15.00 | 2.00 | 30.00 |
| University law library | 28.00 | 10.00 | 2.00 | 90.00 |
| Courthouse library | 16.67 | 20.00 | 10.00 | 20.00 |
| Non-Courthouse government agency nonprofit or international agency law library | 5.50 | 5.50 | 1.00 | 10.00 |

Table 16.3.3 How many subscriptions that require payment does the library maintain to legal journals in both print and electronic access format? Broken out by FTE employees

| FTE employees | Mean | Median | Minimum | Maximum |
|---|---|---|---|---|
| Less than 3 | 15.67 | 15.00 | 2.00 | 30.00 |
| 3 - 4 | 21.50 | 21.50 | 20.00 | 23.00 |
| 5 - 8 | 7.40 | 10.00 | 2.00 | 10.00 |
| More than 8 | 30.25 | 15.00 | 1.00 | 90.00 |

Table 16.3.4 How many subscriptions that require payment does the library maintain to legal journals in both print and electronic access format? Broken out by Current operating status of the library

| Current operating status of the library | Mean | Median | Minimum | Maximum |
|---|---|---|---|---|
| We have completely shut the library | 10.00 | 10.00 | 10.00 | 10.00 |
| We have shut the library to physical traffic but have maintained online access | 18.30 | 10.00 | 1.00 | 90.00 |
| We have kept the library open to patrons subject to social distancing and other virus containment measures | 12.50 | 12.50 | 2.00 | 23.00 |
| We have not really made any major changes in terms of patron access | 30.00 | 30.00 | 30.00 | 30.00 |

## Table 17 How much did (will) the library spend (in US $) for print and/or electronic versions of legal, scientific and other scholarly and professional journals in:

### Table 17.1.1 How much did the library spend (in US $) for print and/or electronic versions of legal, scientific and other scholarly and professional journals in 2019?

| | Mean | Median | Minimum | Maximum |
|---|---|---|---|---|
| Entire sample | 127327.50 | 13965.00 | 0.00 | 700000.00 |

### Table 17.1.2 How much did the library spend (in US $) for print and/or electronic versions of legal, scientific and other scholarly and professional journals in 2019? Broken out by Type of law library

| Type of law library | Mean | Median | Minimum | Maximum |
|---|---|---|---|---|
| Law firm library | 184250.00 | 108000.00 | 0.00 | 521000.00 |
| University law library | 180750.00 | 10250.00 | 2500.00 | 700000.00 |
| Courthouse library | 27500.00 | 27500.00 | 5000.00 | 50000.00 |
| Non-Courthouse government agency nonprofit or international agency law library | 6465.00 | 6465.00 | 1000.00 | 11930.00 |

Table 17.1.3 How much did the library spend (in US $) for print and/or electronic versions of legal, scientific and other scholarly and professional journals in 2019? Broken out by FTE employees

| FTE employees | Mean | Median | Minimum | Maximum |
|---|---|---|---|---|
| Less than 3 | 25000.00 | 25000.00 | 0.00 | 50000.00 |
| 3 - 4 | 360500.00 | 360500.00 | 200000.00 | 521000.00 |
| 5 - 8 | 9750.00 | 9250.00 | 2500.00 | 18000.00 |
| More than 8 | 179482.50 | 8465.00 | 1000.00 | 700000.00 |

Table 17.1.4 How much did the library spend (in US $) for print and/or electronic versions of legal, scientific and other scholarly and professional journals in 2019? Broken out by Current operating status of the library

| Current operating status of the library | Mean | Median | Minimum | Maximum |
|---|---|---|---|---|
| We have completely shut the library | 2500.00 | 2500.00 | 2500.00 | 2500.00 |
| We have shut the library to physical traffic but have maintained online access | 111603.33 | 16000.00 | 1000.00 | 700000.00 |
| We have kept the library open to patrons subject to social distancing and other virus containment measures | 521000.00 | 521000.00 | 521000.00 | 521000.00 |
| We have not really made any major changes in terms of patron access | 0.00 | 0.00 | 0.00 | 0.00 |

Table 17.2.1 How much will the library spend (in US $) for print and/or electronic versions of legal, scientific and other scholarly and professional journals in 2020 (anticipated)?

| | Mean | Median | Minimum | Maximum |
|---|---|---|---|---|
| Entire sample | 110772.08 | 13132.50 | 0.00 | 545000.00 |

Table 17.2.2 How much will the library spend (in US $) for print and/or electronic versions of legal, scientific and other scholarly and professional journals in 2020 (anticipated)? Broken out by Type of law library

| Type of law library | Mean | Median | Minimum | Maximum |
|---|---|---|---|---|
| Law firm library | 183500.00 | 94500.00 | 0.00 | 545000.00 |
| University law library | 130500.00 | 10000.00 | 2000.00 | 500000.00 |
| Courthouse library | 30000.00 | 30000.00 | 10000.00 | 50000.00 |
| Non-Courthouse government agency nonprofit or international agency law library | 6632.50 | 6632.50 | 1000.00 | 12265.00 |

Table 17.2.3 How much will the library spend (in US $) for print and/or electronic versions of legal, scientific and other scholarly and professional journals in 2020 (anticipated)? Broken out by FTE employees

| FTE employees | Mean | Median | Minimum | Maximum |
|---|---|---|---|---|
| Less than 3 | 25000.00 | 25000.00 | 0.00 | 50000.00 |
| 3 - 4 | 360000.00 | 360000.00 | 175000.00 | 545000.00 |
| 5 - 8 | 9000.00 | 8000.00 | 2000.00 | 18000.00 |
| More than 8 | 130816.25 | 11132.50 | 1000.00 | 500000.00 |

Table 17.2.4 How much will the library spend (in US $) for print and/or electronic versions of legal, scientific and other scholarly and professional journals in 2020 (anticipated)? Broken out by Current operating status of the library

| Current operating status of the library | Mean | Median | Minimum | Maximum |
|---|---|---|---|---|
| We have completely shut the library | 2000.00 | 2000.00 | 2000.00 | 2000.00 |
| We have shut the library to physical traffic but have maintained online access | 86918.33 | 14000.00 | 1000.00 | 500000.00 |
| We have kept the library open to patrons subject to social distancing and other virus containment measures | 545000.00 | 545000.00 | 545000.00 | 545000.00 |
| We have not really made any major changes in terms of patron access | 0.00 | 0.00 | 0.00 | 0.00 |

## What are your expectations over the next three years for the library's print collection of journals and periodicals? Broken out by Type of law library

Law firm library

1) Decrease it.
2) Decline in print, if not a complete removal except for some print-only directories and reference material.
3) Print will be significantly reduced.
4) Considering added a few, but this is very speculative
5) will continue to rely on electronic access with older copies available in print. Will also continue to receive certain journals/periodicals complementary in print
6) Print is going away.
7) We don't currently subscribe to any law journals, just a few newsletters that we are currently getting online during the pandemic and I hope to find a way to keep the online access and cancel the print after the current crisis is over.
8) print has already decreased dramatically over the last 5 yrs - potentially further reductions
9) we've already canceled most print titles so no change
10) Continue to decrease spending on print resources, weeding older print resources
11) We will shift as much as we can to online access only.
12) It will get smaller.
13) can't say

University law library

1) We will further reduce subscriptions of print journals and periodicals.
2) About the same, although we will cancel foreign-language materials.
3) Cancelled print journals several years ago. No plans to add any print.
4) It has decreased significantly over the last five years and in the next three years, it may be only 15% of the overall collection.
5) Over the course of the last 20 years, our electronic subscriptions have grown while print decreases, and that pattern will continue but at a somewhat heightened rate.
6) I expect we will migrate many to an online format availability.
7) Decrease subs

Courthouse library

1) Print will be gone.
2) Will be slowly eliminated
3) We have very few print journals/periodicals, so I see perhaps some more cancellations of print, but we have already shifted to digital for the most part for these resources.
4) Unknown at this time.
5) They will be reduced as our budget will be impacted by the COVID-19 pandemic and state funds will be impacted.
6) Likely stay the same or decrease slightly. We canceled almost all of our print journals in favor of access via Hein Online. Those we kept are jurisdictional specific or topically relevant to issues in our state.

Non-Courthouse government agency nonprofit or international agency law library

1) Stay the same or be further reduced. We expect that little will be available in print in the future.
2) Our library subscribes to very few print journals, opting instead for many loose-leaf and annual publications in print format. Over the next three years, we expect to reduce the number of print copies in favour of the digital equivalent.
3) Will be reduced to a small (less than 20) core; Hein Online will satisfy 95% of journal needs

# Table 18 How much did (will) the library spend (in US $) for print reporters in 2019 and 2020?

## Table 18.1.1 How much did the library spend (in US $) for print reporters in 2019?

| | Mean | Median | Minimum | Maximum |
|---|---|---|---|---|
| Entire sample | 47053.85 | 0.00 | 0.00 | 350000.00 |

## Table 18.1.2 How much did the library spend (in US $) for print reporters in 2019? Broken out by Type of law library

| Type of law library | Mean | Median | Minimum | Maximum |
|---|---|---|---|---|
| Law firm library | 1750.00 | 0.00 | 0.00 | 10000.00 |
| University law library | 62500.00 | 0.00 | 0.00 | 250000.00 |
| Courthouse library | 175300.00 | 175300.00 | 600.00 | 350000.00 |
| Non-Courthouse government agency nonprofit or international agency law library | 600.00 | 600.00 | 600.00 | 600.00 |

## Table 18.1.3 How much did the library spend (in US $) for print reporters in 2019? Broken out by FTE employees

| FTE employees | Mean | Median | Minimum | Maximum |
|---|---|---|---|---|
| Less than 3 | 2650.00 | 300.00 | 0.00 | 10000.00 |
| 3 - 4 | 250.00 | 250.00 | 0.00 | 500.00 |
| 5 - 8 | 0.00 | 0.00 | 0.00 | 0.00 |
| More than 8 | 200200.00 | 250000.00 | 600.00 | 350000.00 |

Table 18.1.4 How much did the library spend (in US $) for print reporters in 2019? Broken out by Current operating status of the library

| Current operating status of the library | Mean | Median | Minimum | Maximum |
|---|---|---|---|---|
| We have completely shut the library | 0.00 | 0.00 | 0.00 | 0.00 |
| We have shut the library to physical traffic but have maintained online access | 66855.56 | 500.00 | 0.00 | 350000.00 |
| We have kept the library open to patrons subject to social distancing and other virus containment measures | 0.00 | 0.00 | 0.00 | 0.00 |
| We have not really made any major changes in terms of patron access | 5000.00 | 5000.00 | 0.00 | 10000.00 |

Table 18.2.1 How much will the library spend (in US $) for print reporters in 2020?

| | Mean | Median | Minimum | Maximum |
|---|---|---|---|---|
| Entire sample | 43361.54 | 0.00 | 0.00 | 400000.00 |

Table 18.2.2 How much will the library spend (in US $) for print reporters in 2020? Broken out by Type of law library

| Type of law library | Mean | Median | Minimum | Maximum |
|---|---|---|---|---|
| Law firm library | 2083.33 | 0.00 | 0.00 | 12000.00 |
| University law library | 37500.00 | 0.00 | 0.00 | 150000.00 |
| Courthouse library | 200300.00 | 200300.00 | 600.00 | 400000.00 |
| Non-Courthouse government agency nonprofit or international agency law library | 600.00 | 600.00 | 600.00 | 600.00 |

Table 18.2.3 How much will the library spend (in US $) for print reporters in 2020? Broken out by FTE employees

| FTE employees | Mean | Median | Minimum | Maximum |
|---|---|---|---|---|
| Less than 3 | 3150.00 | 300.00 | 0.00 | 12000.00 |
| 3 - 4 | 250.00 | 250.00 | 0.00 | 500.00 |
| 5 - 8 | 0.00 | 0.00 | 0.00 | 0.00 |
| More than 8 | 183533.33 | 150000.00 | 600.00 | 400000.00 |

Table 18.2.4 How much will the library spend (in US $) for print reporters in 2020? Broken out by Current operating status of the library

| Current operating status of the library | Mean | Median | Minimum | Maximum |
|---|---|---|---|---|
| We have completely shut the library | 0.00 | 0.00 | 0.00 | 0.00 |
| We have shut the library to physical traffic but have maintained online access | 61300.00 | 500.00 | 0.00 | 400000.00 |
| We have kept the library open to patrons subject to social distancing and other virus containment measures | 0.00 | 0.00 | 0.00 | 0.00 |
| We have not really made any major changes in terms of patron access | 6000.00 | 6000.00 | 0.00 | 12000.00 |

## In general, how has the coronavirus epidemic impacted or will impact your print materials collection? Broken out by Type of law library

Law firm library

1) See the answer regarding intake above
2) We are almost entirely electronic so minimal impact.
3) We will question the need to hold anything in print that is available electronically.
4) We will likely reduce the number of active print reporter subscriptions
5) we have asked for shipments to be held. However, once the restrictions are lifted we plan to accept those delayed shipments.
6) Yes, because no one is in the office print material is being canceled
7) We have been decreasing our print collection for years. We had some local newspapers and newsletters that we have canceled or moved online during the epidemic. Rule books have or will be taken off standing order for now. We keep a few specialty treatises firmwide and may keep those for now. I plan to cancel as much print as I can during the epidemic.
8) further reductions
9) Everything we had been routing in print has been moved to digital wherever possible. No change otherwise because print is already minimal, mainly office copies and a few one-off treatises that either aren't online or are cheaper in print
10) impacted current access as most offices closed or on skeleton staffing; will likely hasten cancellation and weeding decisions
11) It has made the firm rethink whether a primarily physical library is practical going forward. Our firm lawyers never wanted books and newsletters online in the past. Now they requesting online access.
12) It will get smaller.
13) can't say

University law library

1) It will reduce print materials. We will prefer e-book format and will press publishers to provide it.
2) We will reduce print course reserves to reduce F2F transactions at the circulation desk.
3) Eliminated most of the print collection several years ago. Epidemic will not impact our current print materials collection.
4) Less 100,000 in print.
5) It's certainly impacted access to the collection

6) Yes. We will continue to weed and reduce our print collection where appropriately.
7) We have a lot of unprocessed materials building up in our building while we're under lockdown.
8) Not used print. Will spend more on e-resources

Courthouse library

1) Print will be gone.
2) Will slowly disappear
3) It may allow us to introduce or re-introduce online counterparts to users and, eventually, allow us to cancel some more of our print collection.
4) Reduced our income; we may have to cut back on all print subscriptions.
5) The pandemic will undoubtedly affect our budget as we are a state funded law library. Incoming revenue is sure to be less than it was in a pre-COVID 19 environment.
6) I was looking to cut a major chunk of our print collection even before the pandemic, but the fact that it hasn't been clamored for during our closure is great evidence that I can likely move more content online and gut the print collection. This includes our reporter collection--we are likely one of the few law libraries left that still gets EVERY reporter in existence (except the Federal Appendix and I'm not sure why we don't because we get everything else!).

Non-Courthouse government agency nonprofit or international agency law library

1) The lost revenue from court filing fees will likely result in further cuts to print. Also, we are uncertain if users will want to handle circulating materials in print in the future.
2) Because it has only been two months since the library has been inaccessible, we have opted to continue receiving our print subscriptions and standing orders. As for monographs, purchasing of print books has been put on hold for the foreseeable future.
3) Will accelerate the cancelling of print materials, especially when there are electronic alternatives with exactly the same content

Made in United States
Orlando, FL
04 November 2026

90208074R00077